CUBA '62

Tourist attractions
of the island,
early 1950s

►► **Overleaf**

Defence of the island,
constant since the time of
the Bay of Pigs invasion
photo: © Andrew St. George

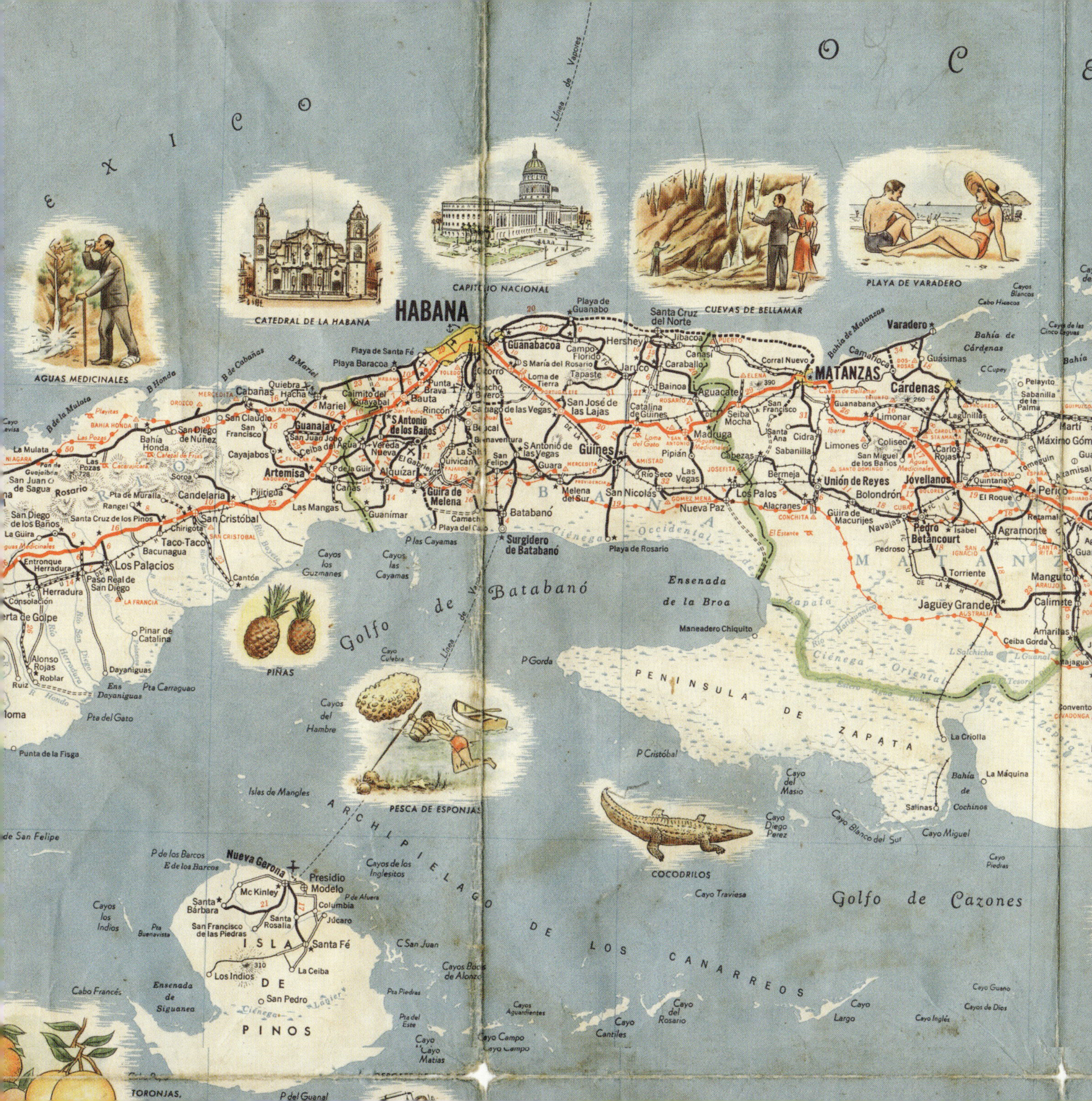
O C É
GOLFO DE MEXICO
AGUAS MEDICINALES
CATEDRAL DE LA HABANA
CAPITOLIO NACIONAL
CUEVAS DE BELLAMAR
PLAYA DE VARADERO
HABANA
Varadero
Bahía de Cárdenas
MATANZAS
Cárdenas
Bahía de Matanzas
Guanabacoa
Santa Cruz del Norte
Playa de Guanabo
Hershey
Campo Florido
Sta María del Rosario
Jaruco
Canasí
Caraballo
Bainoa
Aguacate
Corral Nuevo
Limonar
Guanabana
Contreras
Máximo Góm
Playa de Santa Fé
Playa Baracoa
Morro
Punta Brava
Loma de Tierra
Tapaste
San José de las Lajas
Catalina de Güines
Seiba Mocha
San Francisco
Santa Ana
Cidra
Limones
Coliseo
Carlos Rojas
Sabanilla de la Palma
B Honda
Cabañas
Quiebra Hacha
Mariel
Calimito de Guayabal
Bauta
Rincón
Santiago de las Vegas
Madruga
Cabezas
Sabanilla
Unión de Reyes
Jovellanos
Quintana
San Claudio
San Francisco
GUANAJAY
San Juan Jobo
S ANTONIO de los Baños
Vereda Nueva
El Gabriel
La Salud
Buenaventura
S Antonio de las Vegas
Guara
GÜINES
Pipián
Río Seco
Las Vegas
Bermeja
Bolondrón
El Roque
Bahía Honda
Soroa
Candelaria
ARTEMISA
Pijirigua
Las Mangas
Cañas
Güira de Melena
Guanímar
Alquízar
San Felipe
Melena del Sur
San Nicolás
Los Palos
Alacranes
Güira de Macurijes
Navajas
Pedro Betancourt
Isabel
Agramonte
San Diego de Núñez
Cayajabos
P de la Güira
Batabanó
Nueva Paz
Pedroso
Los Palacios
San Cristóbal
Taco-Taco
Bacunagua
Cantón
Surgidero de Batabanó
Playa de Rosario
Jagüey Grande
Torriente
Manguito
Calimete
Amarillas
Ceiba Gorda
Pinar de Catalina
PIÑAS
Cayo Culebra
Golfo de Batabanó
Ensenada de la Broa
Maneadero Chiquito
P Gorda
PENÍNSULA DE ZAPATA
Ciénega Oriental
La Criolla
Cayos del Hambre
PESCA DE ESPONJAS
Islas de Mangles
P Cristóbal
Cayo del Masio
Bahía de Cochinos
La Máquina
Salinas
ARCHIPIÉLAGO DE LOS CANARREOS
Cayo Diego Perez
Cayo Blanco del Sur
Cayo Miguel
COCODRILOS
Golfo de Cazones
Nueva Gerona
Presidio Modelo
Mc Kinley
Columbia
Santa Bárbara
Santa Rosalía
Júcaro
San Francisco de las Piedras
Santa Fé
ISLA DE PINOS
Los Indios
La Ceiba
San Pedro
Cayo Traviesa
Cayos de los Inglesitos
C San Juan
Cayos Bacis de Alonzo
Cayos Aguardientes
Cayo del Rosario
Cayo Largo
Cayo Guano
Cayos de Dios
Cayo Inglés
TORONJAS

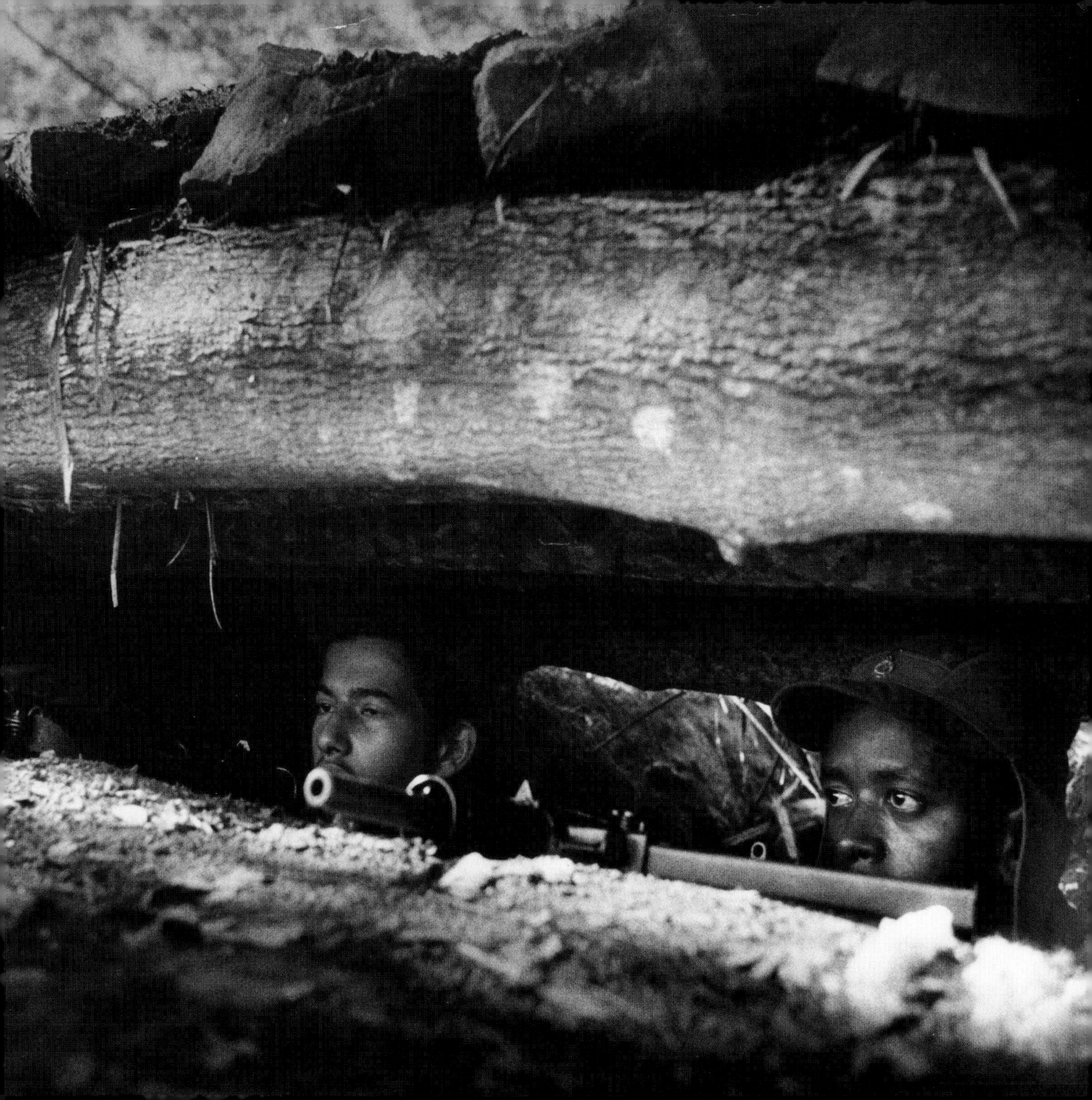

Richard Hollis and JS Tennant

CUBA '62

Preludes to a World Crisis

Five Leaves

Five Leaves Publications
14a Long Row, Nottingham NG1 2DH
www.fiveleaves.co.uk

First published in Great Britain
by Five Leaves Publications 2022
Copyright © Richard Hollis & JS Tennant, September 2022
Richard Hollis & JS Tennant assert their moral right
to be identified as the authors of this work
in accordance with the
Copyright, Designs and Patents Act 1988

ISBN: 9781910170991

Design and layout by Richard Hollis
Printed in Great Britain by
Short Run Press, Exeter

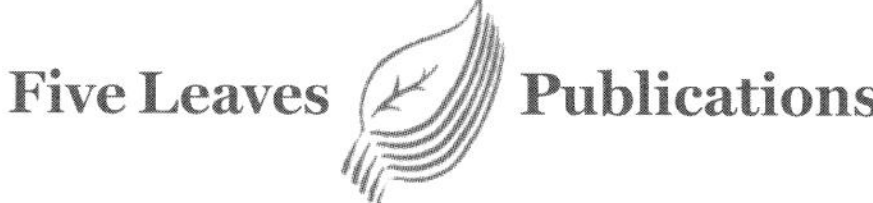

PREFACE

This book came about through a chance meeting of two people, of different generations, with very different experiences of Cuba.

Richard Hollis spent a month on the island in 1962; his diaries, letters and photographs were the inspiration behind this collage of texts and images which all, loosely, relate to that year. Without, of course, realising the significance, he saw groups of Soviet soldiers dressed as farmworkers in check shirts while in the Cuban countryside. Tourism, in the conventional sense, had disappeared not long after the 1959 Revolution: it may be that Hollis – however inadvertently – was the only visitor to witness the covert build-up of Russian forces that summer.

JS Tennant has been travelling to Cuba regularly for twenty years. He was among the first foreigners to visit the Soviet bases used during the Missile Crisis, notably UEB El Cacho (known to the CIA as 'San Cristóbal 1') which was until recently in use by Cuban special forces and remains off-limits to the public.

The colour photographs in *Cuba '62*, unless stated otherwise, date from a six-month period he spent living on the island in 2010. All uncredited black-and-white photographs are by Richard Hollis. Translations, including from the script of *Memories of Underdevelopment* and the novel by Edmundo Desnoes on which the film is based, are by Tennant.

The versions of texts by Juan Goytisolo, starting on p.21, are excerpted from *Pueblo en marcha* ('A People on the Move'), a Cuban travelogue from early 1962 not, until now, available in English.

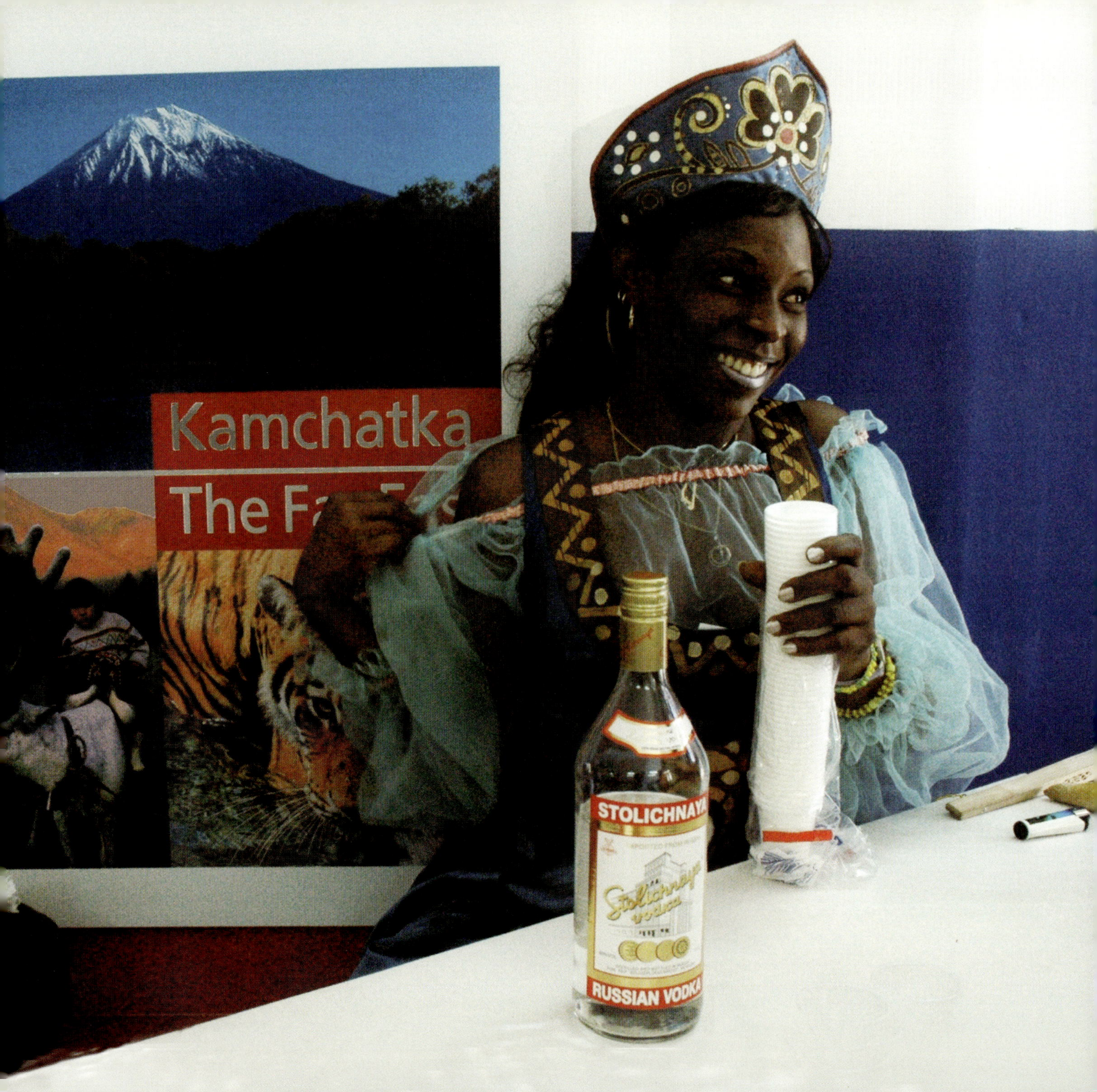
Kamchatka
The Fa[r] E[as]t
STOLICHNAYA
IMPORTED FROM RUSSIA
Stolichnaya
vodka
RUSSIAN VODKA

Cuban woman
serves vodka:
Russian trade fair,
La Cabaña fortress,
Havana

PRELUDE
JS Tennant

Cuba's history in the first half of the twentieth century is one of a country debased by a string of caudillo-style dictators, most of whom were propped up by US interests (if not the US government itself) and each, seemingly, more corrupt and bloodthirsty than the last. Cuban hopes for sovereignty and freedom – after victory over Spain in 1898, following a drawn-out war – were stymied by concessions demanded by their neighbour to the north for the decisive part they played in that defeat. After four hundred years of Spanish rule Cuba became, in all but name, a colony of the US.

By the 1950s the US was investing $713 million annually in Havana, but almost entirely in the service sector. A crackdown on gambling in that decade routed much of it into the island, and the Cuban president – General Fulgencio Batista – went as far as to employ the US mafia boss Meyer Lansky as an advisor on urban planning. The Nicaraguan poet and revolutionary Ernesto Cardenal noted that, at the Hotel Capri (controlled by the mobster Santo Trafficante, Jr.), visiting US businessmen could request a woman to be included with their room reservation. Lansky designed and financed the Hotel Riviera, which when it opened was the largest casino hotel in the world

Fidel's brother, Raúl Castro,
brandishing photograph
of masked fighter,
Santiago de Cuba
photo © Andrew St. George

outside of Las Vegas. Such was the urban scene in the years during which Fidel Castro's rebel army was waging a nationalist guerrilla campaign from the mountains. His forces finally took over the country, Batista having fled, on 1 January 1959.

Nikita Khrushchev – most arbitrary and unpredictable of statesmen – rose to power on a tide of increased agricultural prosperity following his consolidation of Stalin's confused system of collective farming. Following the ruler's death, having won over the Central Committee, Khrushchev became First Secretary of the Communist Party of the Soviet Union in 1953. He was involved in the purges in Ukraine, yet delivered a notorious secret speech criticising Stalin – a man who would delight in forcing Khrushchev to dance the Ukrainian hopak after dinner – to the Twentieth Party Congress in 1956. By the Twenty-Second Congress, in 1961, it had been agreed that Stalin's embalmed corpse should be removed from where it lay in Lenin's mausoleum in Red Square.

The first year of the Cuban Revolution saw the beginnings of an agrarian reform that reduced all estates to one thousand acres, redistributing any excess without compensation to landowners.

In February 1960, a Russian technical and trade fair was opened in Havana by Soviet Deputy Premier Anastas Mikoyan, who would soon play a key role in the Cuban Missile Crisis. Cubans flocked to the fair, marvelling at replicas of Sputnik, the first space satellite; model homes; at factories and farming equipment that Khrushchev boasted would soon 'bury' the West. This was the nation, after all, that had put a dog into orbit.

The USSR publicly announced that it would purchase a million tonnes of sugar from Cuba over the next four years; formal diplomatic relations were established between the two countries. Fidel Castro made his first request for Soviet arms and, in June 1960, a shipment of oil, tanks, anti-aircraft guns and artillery, along with technical advisors, arrived. The following month, all US-owned businesses were nationalised, again without compensation. President Eisenhower cut Cuba's sugar quota and threatened further sanctions. Unidentified aeroplanes began to appear in the skies above the island, dropping incendiary bombs on cane fields and sugar mills.

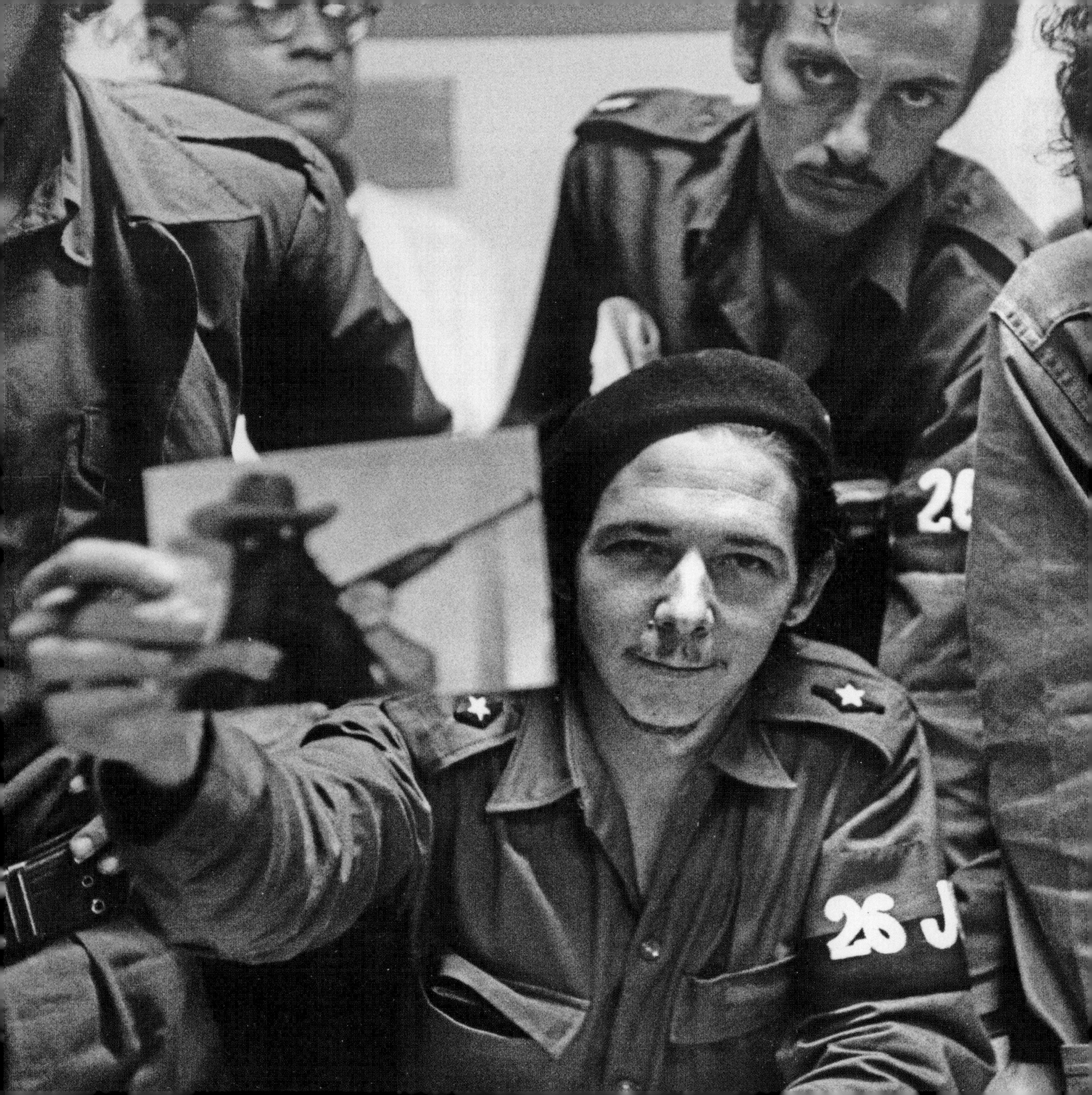

In September 1960, Cuba created the Committees for the Defence of the Revolution (CDRs) in the Soviet mould of democratic centralism. The CDRs were a nationwide network of civic organisations led by one representative from each block, or street, tasked with ensuring revolutionary decrees were implemented, offenders reported on.

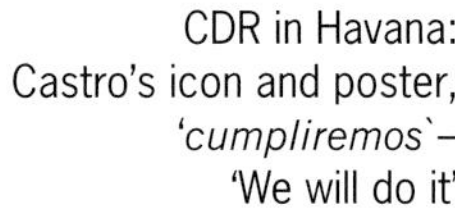

CDR in Havana:
Castro's icon and poster,
'cumpliremos` –
'We will do it'

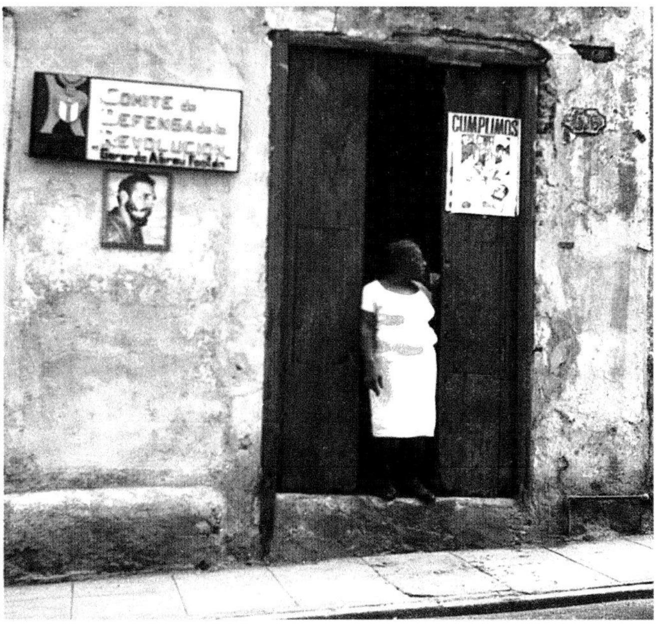

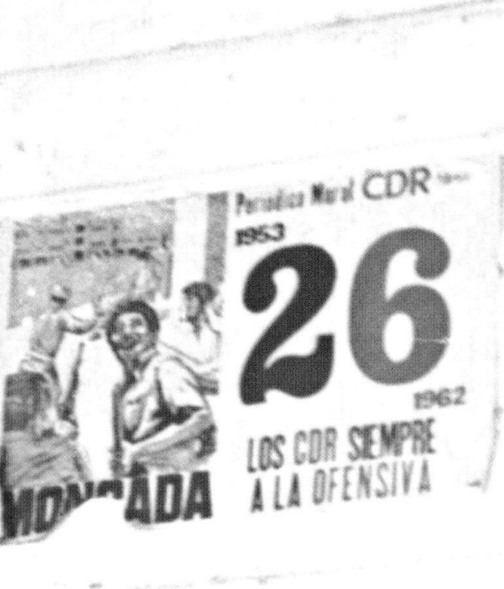

Periódico Mural CDR
1953
26
1962
LOS CDR SIEMPRE
A LA OFENSIVA
MONCADA

CDR
CON LA GUARDIA
EN ALTO
SERGIO GONSALEZ
(EL CURITA)

The question of Cuba – then, as now, a defining issue of US domestic, as much as foreign, policy – became a key topic in presidential election campaigning between Richard Nixon and John F. Kennedy. In October 1960, while Ernesto 'Che' Guevara and Mikoyan attended a performance at the Bolshoi Theatre in Moscow, the USA imposed a trade embargo on Cuba still in force at the time of writing: the longest such embargo in history.

Diplomatic relations with the US were severed at the start of 1961, and American citizens prohibited from entering the island a few days later. The learning of English began to be discouraged in Cuba with that of Russian promoted in its place. More and more Soviet Bloc workers travelled to the Caribbean island, astonished at the new TVs still in the shops, the taste of Coca-Cola, garish US road-cruisers fangled with tail-fins and leather trim. Cubans became so perturbed by the personal hygiene of their new guests – namely the absence of deodorant – that Che Guevara felt obliged to comment on it on national television: *New times call for new sacrifices.*

Relief sculpture on pillar, Vedado district of Havana, marks the spot where Castro announced the socialist nature of the revolution

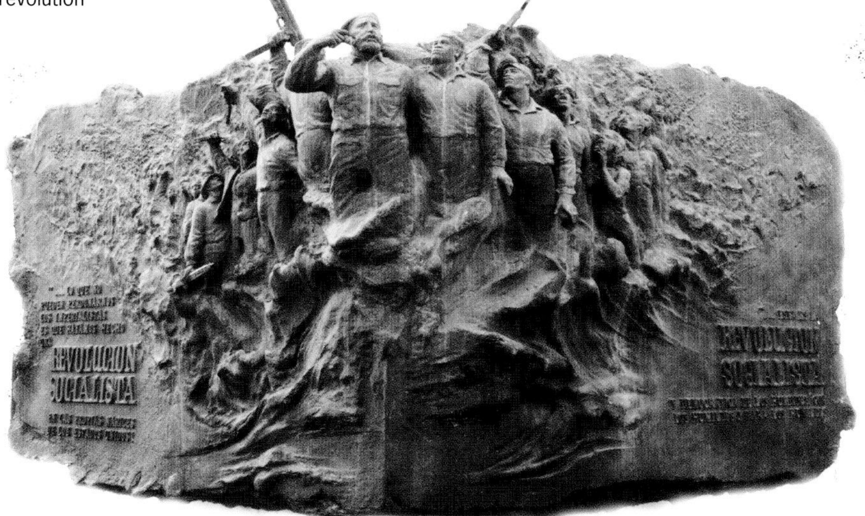

In the spring, a CIA-backed invasion of Cuba was turned back and humiliated at the Bay of Pigs, with over a thousand mercenaries taken prisoner. In the wake of the attack, Fidel Castro proclaimed the socialist nature of his government for the first time. Khrushchev, wary of Castro's assertion, refused to be drawn publicly on the subject.

On 23 April 1961, Havana's El Encanto (one of the largest department stores in the Americas) was burnt to the ground with a phosphorous bomb in the days after it had been nationalised. At the May Day rally in the Plaza de la Revolución (until recently the Plaza Cívica), hundreds of thousands of Cubans joined to sing the Internationale.

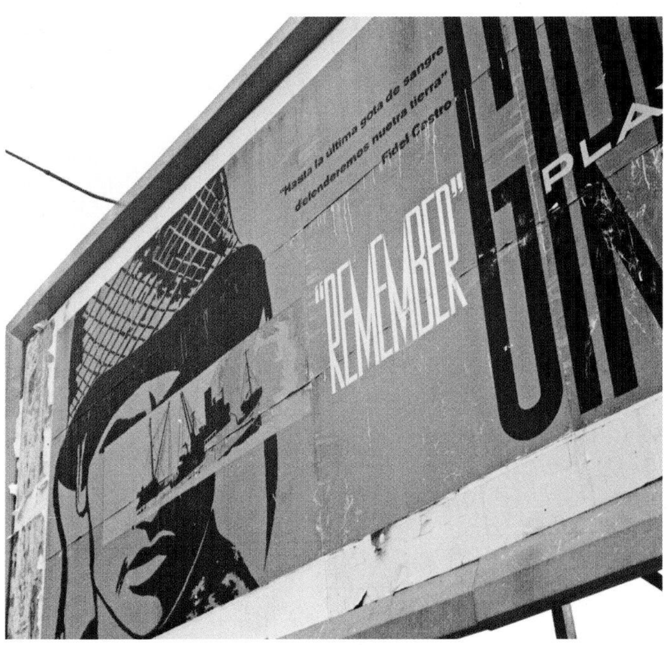

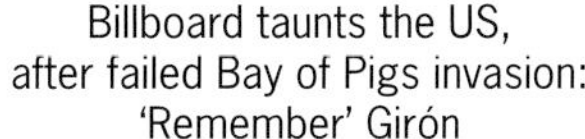
Billboard taunts the US,
after failed Bay of Pigs invasion:
'Remember' Girón

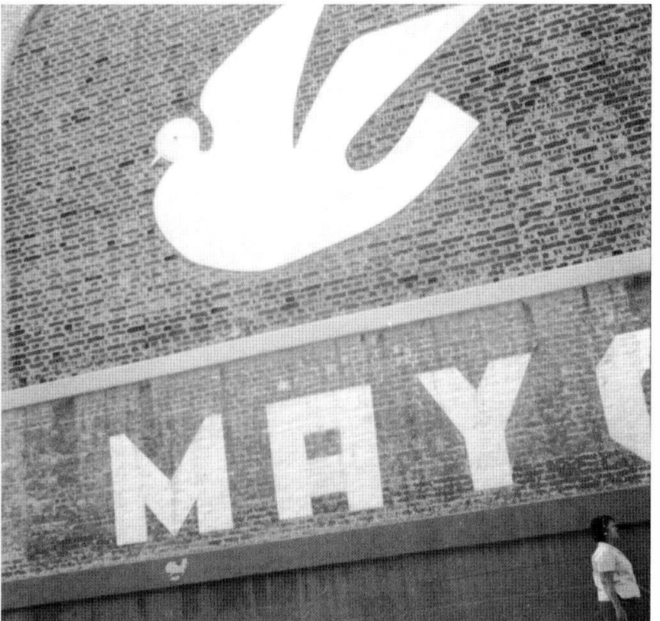

'We will do it It!' handbook
issued to Conrado Benítez literacy brigade
June 1961

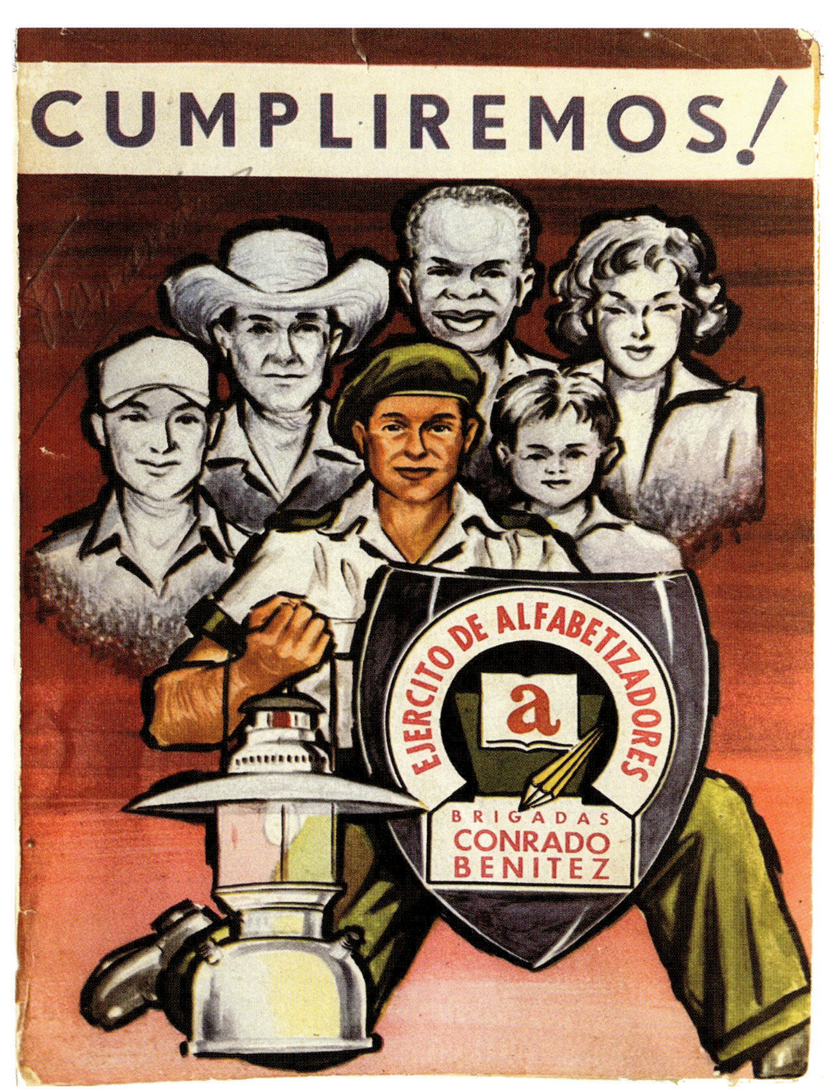

CUMPLIREMOS!
EJERCITO DE ALFABETIZADORES
a
BRIGADAS
CONRADO
BENITEZ

In 1959, at the time of the Revolution, only fifty per cent of Cuban children were enrolled in school and, among peasant families, less than half of adults had received any education. While urban illiteracy rates were comparable to other Latin American countries, in rural areas they stood at around forty per cent. The government declared 1961 the Year of Literacy, calling for teachers and volunteers to go out into the country and up into the high sierras. 100,000 schoolchildren, some as young as ten years old, volunteered to become literacy *brigadistas*, brigade members, as did a further 150,000 volunteer teachers, known as *alfabetizadores*. Youth were formed into the Conrado Benítez Brigade, named for a black teenager who was tortured and murdered while working on a pilot literacy programme in the mountains.

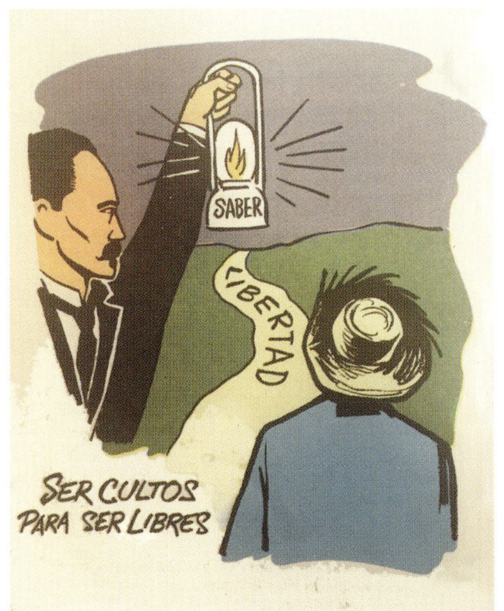

'Freedom through education.'

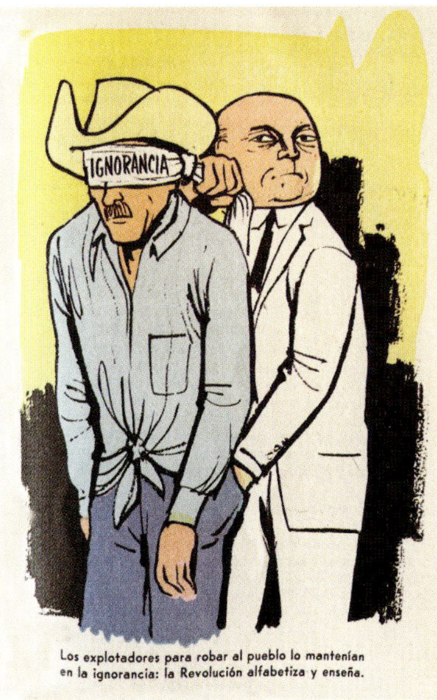

'To rob the people, the overlords kept them in a state of ignorance. The Revolution brings literacy and teaches.'

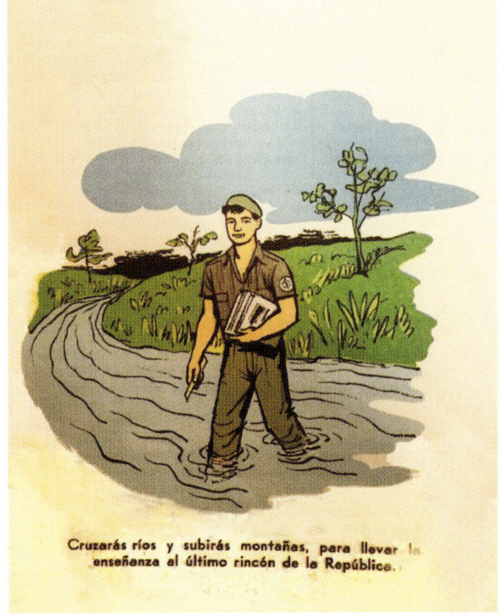

'You will ford rivers and scale mountains to bring teaching to the farthest corners of the republic.'

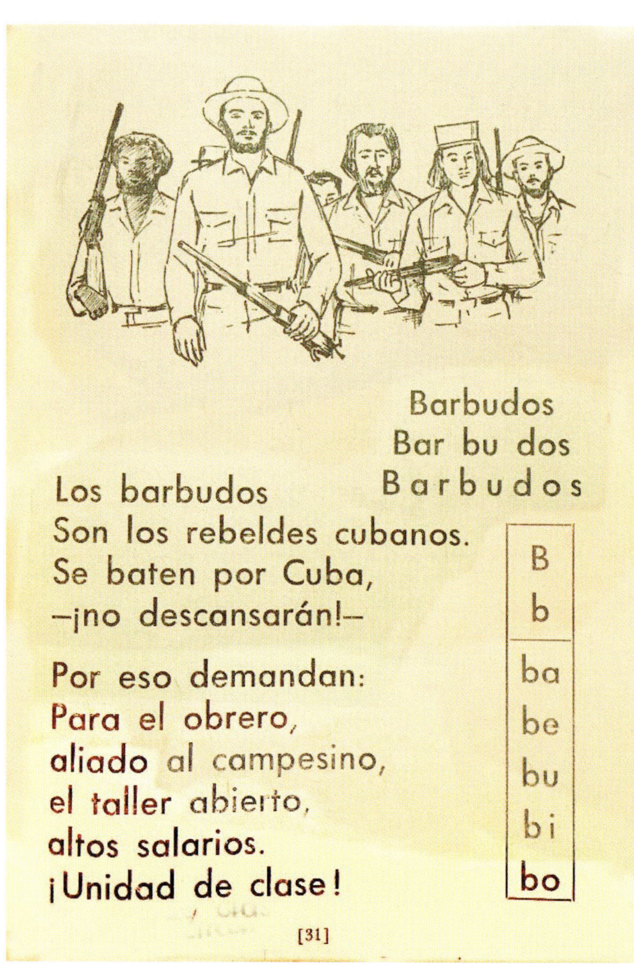

Page from revolutionary
spelling manual

Many were away from home for as long as eight months, roving around the country, lodging with those whom they were teaching to read and write. Each *brigadista* was given a primer and teacher's manual, two books, two pairs of socks, an olive-green beret, a hammock. 'Chinese' lanterns were distributed from a shipment of paraffin lamps gifted by the People's Republic of China. Topic Two in the standard issue instruction manual read:

Fidel is Our Leader. We Cubans respect and love the leader who called the people to arms against tyranny and foreign domination. We respect and love those who guide us in the fight to make Cuba free.

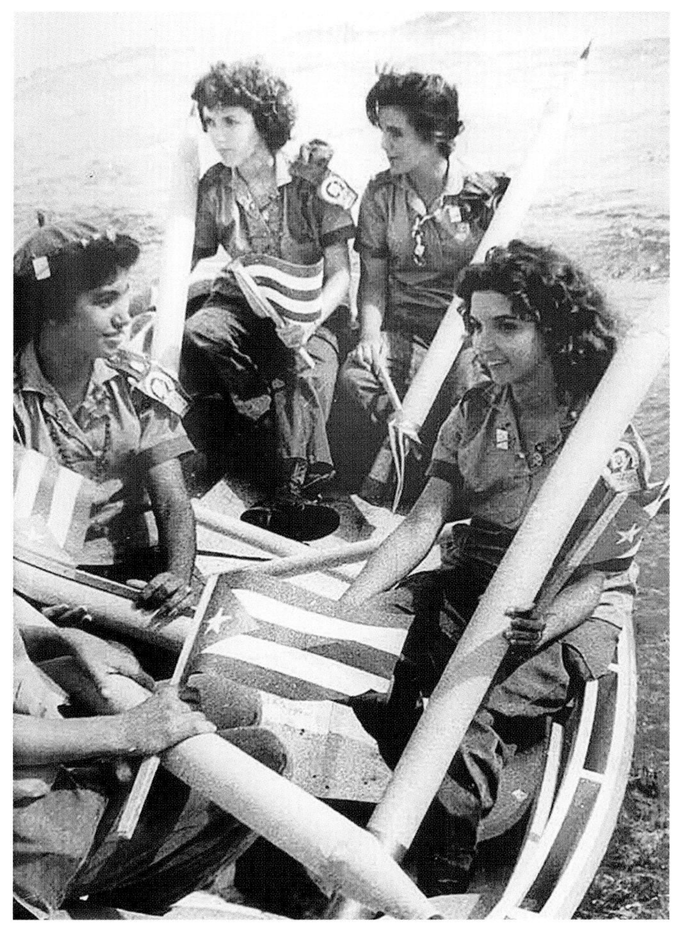

Second Bay of Pigs invasion:
brigadistas armed with pencils

Illiteracy was framed as an occupying force to be conquered. A mock re-invasion was staged at the Bay of Pigs: young women in rowing boats, not amphibious landing craft, came ashore with giant pencils in the crooks of their arms in place of rifles.

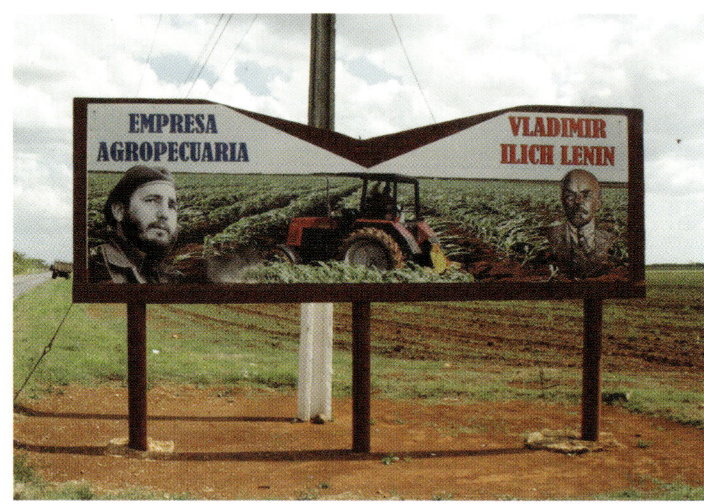

Vladimir Ilich Lenin collective farm, Matanzas Province

After the Bay of Pigs misadventure, fearing the Cuban revolutionary blueprint would be exported to other countries, the US began funding various counter-insurgency programmes across Latin America. In November, the CIA was granted fifty million dollars per annum to run covert operations aimed at destabilising Cuba. Around the same time the American Jupiter missiles, installed in Italy and Turkey earlier in the year – within range of Moscow – became fully operational. These nuclear-tipped, medium-range, weapons had been designed by Wernher von Braun, Hitler's rocket expert who was one of the founders of the American missile programme.

The CIA was unaware that the Soviets – despite propaganda such as Khrushchev's assertion that their weapons could 'knock a fly out of the sky' – barely had any long-range missiles capable of reaching the US. The Jupiters, for the Russians, represented a significant tipping of the balance with regards to the 'missile gap' that so obsessed both nations. The following month Castro, out of exigency and design, clarified he was a full-blown communist of the Soviet stripe: 'I am a Marxist-Leninist, and I shall be a Marxist-Leninist to the end of my life'.

'62

31 JANUARY. Under pressure from the US, Cuba is expelled from the Organization of American States (OAS).

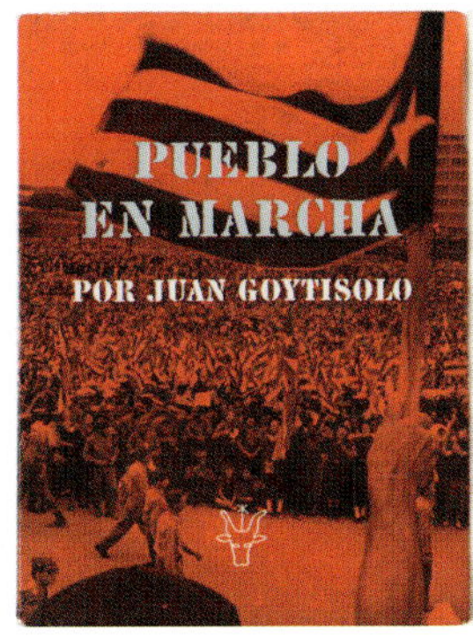

Writing by
Juan Goytisolo
pp.21-33

When I landed at the airport in Havana, the successive images of my childhood, adolescence and youth melted away when faced with a people that the Revolution had set in motion ... The landing of the *Granma* [the yacht the Castros and their men arrived in], the battles in the Sierra, jolted me out of my apathy. There was a curse that seemed to weigh upon our Spanish-speaking nations, forever asleep, forever immobile as if flattened beneath the weight of oligarchies and caste.

Parque de la Fraternidad, Havana

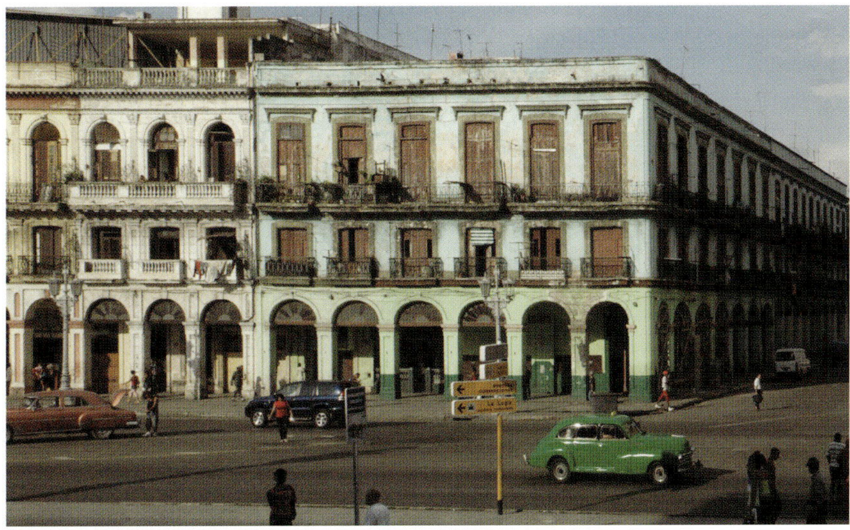

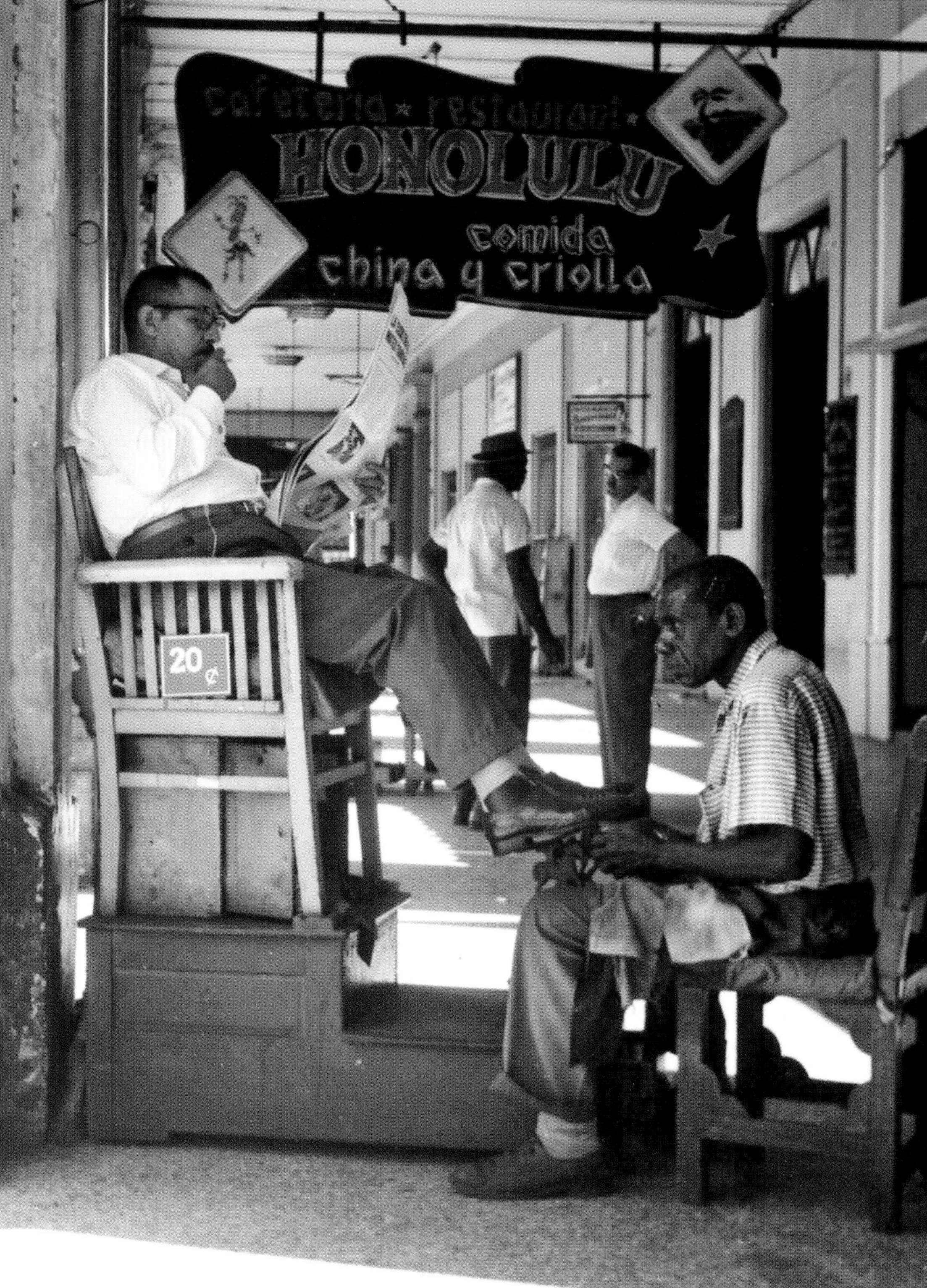
GRAN
AMERICA
PRADO
-408-
cafeteria * restaurant *
HONOLULU
comida
china y criolla
20¢

Bootblack,
Paseo del Prado, Havana

In the days before my trip to Oriente, I idle under the arcades of Havana's Parque de la Fraternidad, under the onslaught of the vendors, applauding the snake charmer, leafing through the miraculous prayers of the *santeros*. Colour photographs of Fidel and Camilo Cienfuegos alternate with icons of Saint Barbara and the Virgin of El Cobre; the complete works of José Martí, and those of Lenin, with pamphlets on the scientific basis for religion.

Inside the palaces abandoned by the bourgeoisie, thousands of young people study theatre, music and dance. The people irrupt into a precinct sacrosanct to the fantasies and nostalgias of the class into which I was born and, ranged throughout the threadbare salons, photographs of Fidel and Raúl replace old family portraits ... schoolchildren draw Lenin's face – bald, with moustache and goatee. Some round off their work with a cloud or blazing sun that seems to hover above the cranium of the Soviet leader, like a halo.

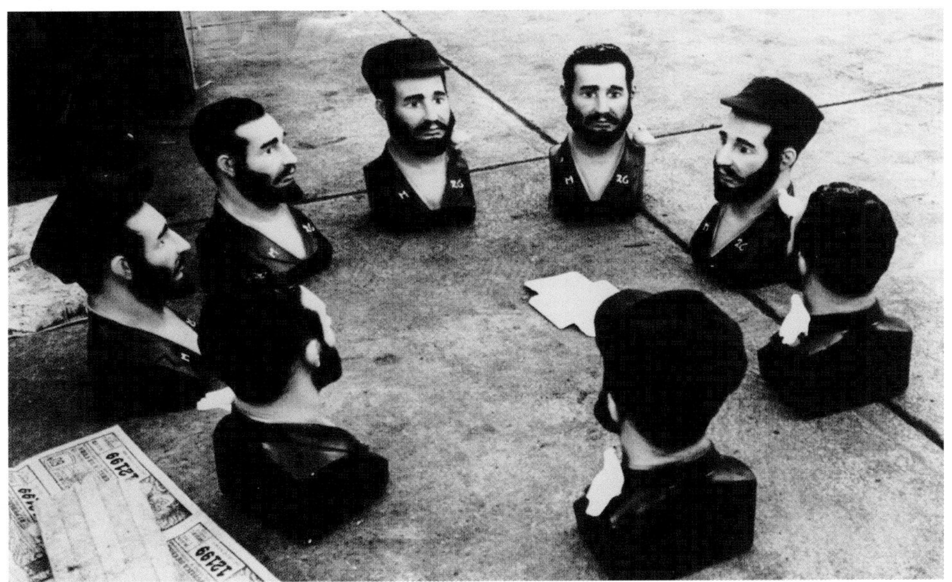

Plaster busts
of Fidel
and lottery tickets.
photo © Andrew
St. George

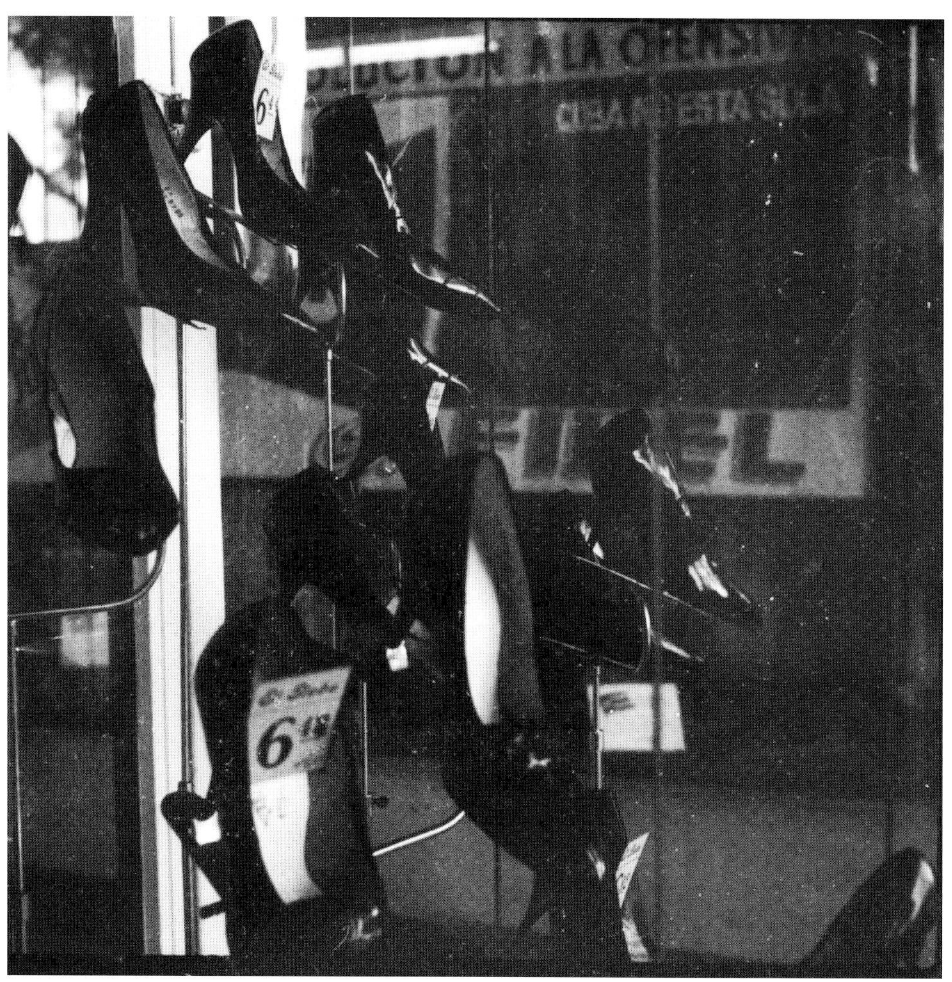

Ladies' shoeshop, Centro Havana

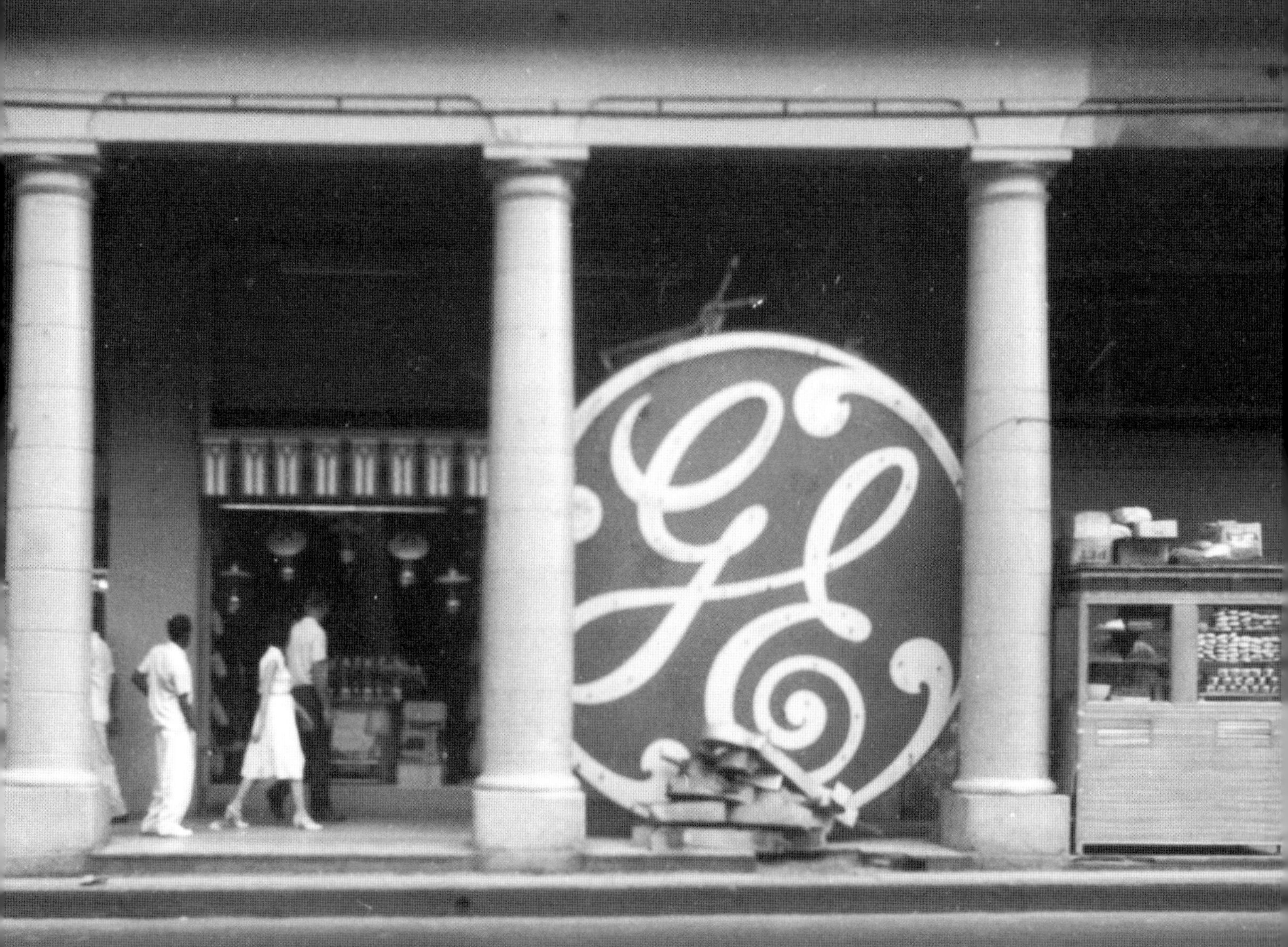

G E

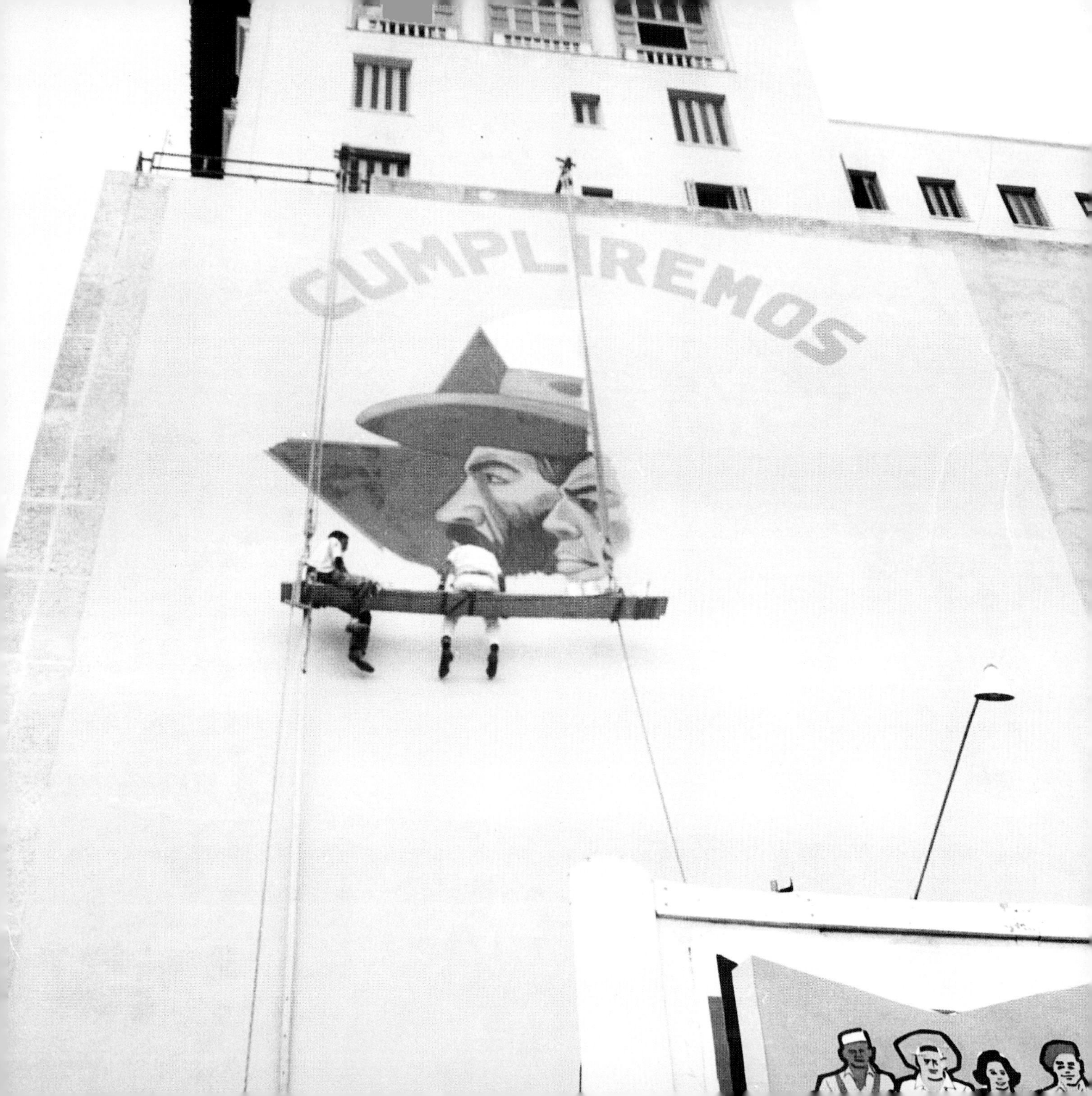

CUMPLIREMOS

Havana port: mural
commemorating
literacy programme

In the villages and hamlets, the *guajiros* loaf around out in front of the state-owned store; Fidel's photo adorns each of their thatched huts and, beside the road, the wooden posts of the INRA [National Institute for Agrarian Reform] - painted orange and white - stretch on for miles and miles. The new housing blocks, the cooperatives, and state-owned stores are rapidly transforming the landscape. Trucks go by loaded with material and, as we approach the foothills of the sierra, the impression of a world being born – offspring of a more just society – comes violently over the traveller.

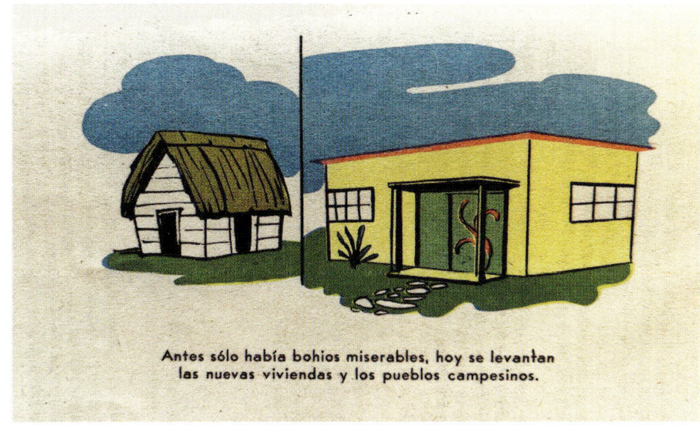

'Before there were only miserable huts, now they're putting up new homes and campesino settlements.'

The city has just been proclaimed a Territory Free of Illiteracy and, as we progress beneath the bunting and triumphal arches, the driver tells me that all the literacy volunteers from the sierra are going to congregate here before they return to Havana … The militiaman says that, until the fall of Batista, he'd lived in ignorance. He knew how to read and write, but didn't understand the meaning of the word 'capitalism', nor the precise meaning of the term 'alienation'.

There is a festive atmosphere across the city, of excitement and joy. In the plaza, the week's programme of events is announced at top volume over a speaker. Everyone hums the anthem of the Conrado Benítez Brigades. A stream of people flows under the arcades, the cafés are packed … Finally, I return to the hotel and go to bed without undressing. I think that, three years after its fall, the tyranny still pains the heart, blood and dignity of the people.

★

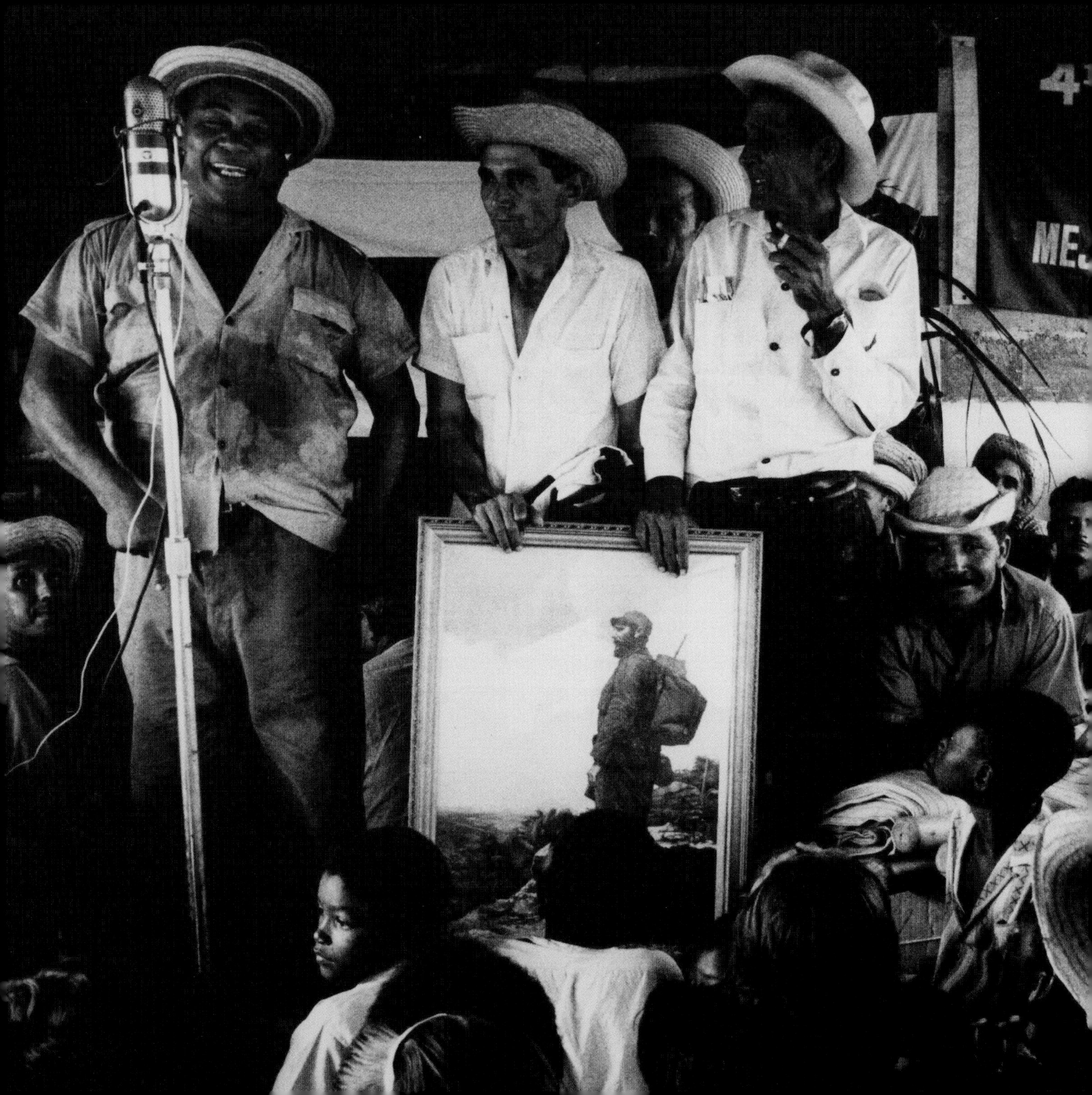
MEJ

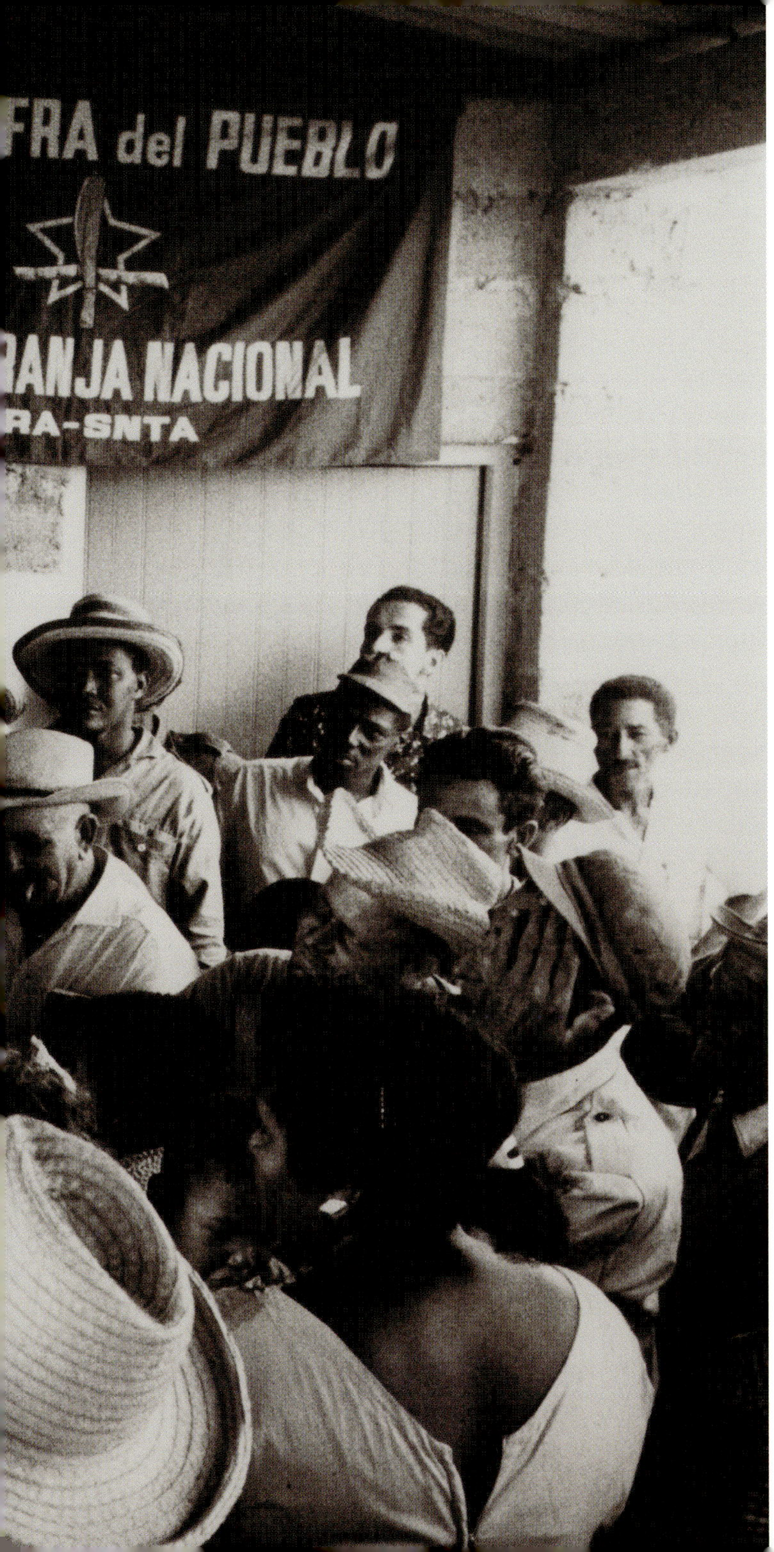

Campesinos celebrate the award
of 'Best Farm'
photo © Luc Chessex

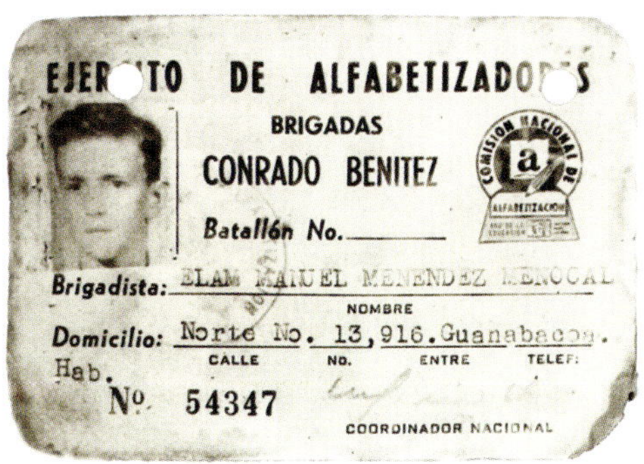

Those of the Patria o Muerte or Conrado Benítez Brigades, volunteer teachers and literacy workers, come in from swampland or highland villages with uncharacteristically long hair, boots white with dust, and sun-worn skin. The majority of the men sport beards and wander in gleeful groups throughout the city, with campesino seed necklaces, a cigar butt between the lips. The girls have not shed their coquettishness, wearing neatly-ironed, clean shirts with a small Cuban flag and photo of Fidel.

Between them the optimism is contagious. Over a period of many months, they have lived far removed from their families and friends, sharing the crude existence of the *guajiros*, charcoal vendors and fishermen, rising with the lark and going to bed at dusk, tormented by the heat, the sandflies and mosquitos. All for the sake of carrying teaching to the hundreds of thousands of souls kept – first by Spanish colonialism, and then, later, by American capital and monopolies – in a state of backwardness and ignorance. Forced to work out in the maize fields, coffee plantations, pasturelands and cattle ranches, sleeping in hammocks and on camp beds, without light except for candles and oil lamps, these men and women are no longer the same as those who set out half a year back from Havana, Pinar del Río or Santiago. If the *guajiros*, charcoal vendors and fishermen no longer stand idly by – offended, frustrated in their dignity as men – they have also acquired a new nobility in relation to their alienated and dispossessed brethren. In the space of a few short months, the Revolution has achieved a moral transformation on a par with that which the traveller notes in the economic realm. Men, asleep for centuries, have woken suddenly to their potential as authentic beings and, in that clash, the literacy teachers have simultaneously purged a large number of old prejudices and selfish traits. A new feeling runs the full length of the island ... the faces of men, women, children and the elderly are lit up, burnished. The heart warms, and happiness pulses in recognition of what this really is: fraternity.

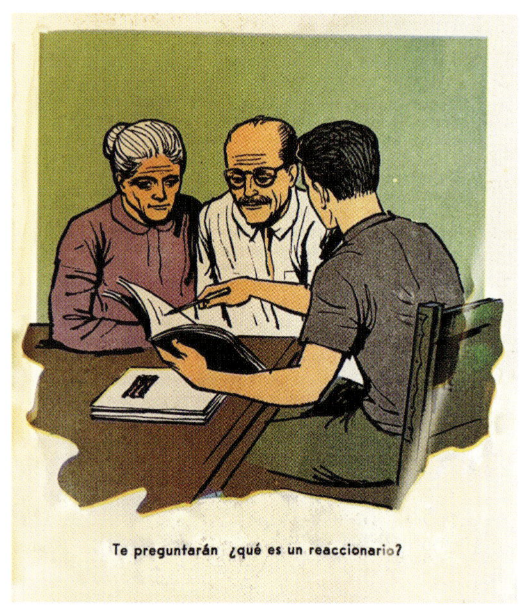

'And they will ask you, Just what is a reactionary?'

12 MARCH Widespread shortages across the island. Rationing on food and other basic goods imposed. 

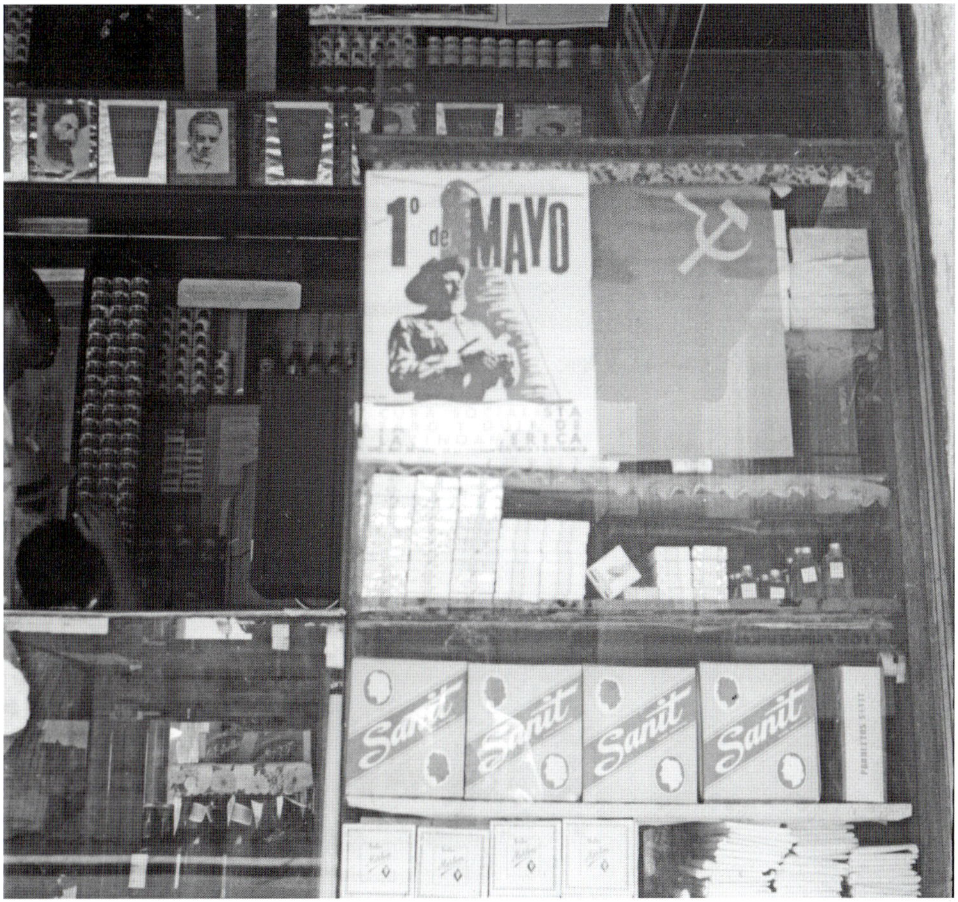

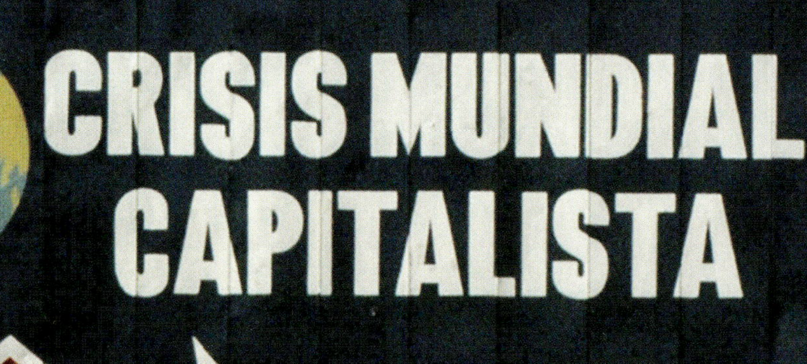
CRISIS MUNDIAL CAPITALISTA
"...No tenemos otra opción que unirnos para enfrentarla".
Raúl Castro

Everyone goes quiet for a while. Bit by bit, the ranks of those surrounding us have swelled. At last, a militiaman unfolds the newspaper he has under his arm and reads some lines from Kennedy's latest speech. 'What do you reckon?', he says. 'The guy always talks as if the world were his alone. It makes you wonder if he's got his head screwed on properly.'
'They'll have their work cut out', says a teacher. 'Kennedy is an imbecile!'

The INRA is building cooperatives, communal housing, technical schools, poultry farms. Soviet and Czechoslovak tractors plough the fields ahead of the next cotton-sowing; mass unemployment is a distant memory, like illiteracy, fear, hunger and persecution.

Come evening, leaning on the counter of some café, I amuse myself by watching the bands of friends and the indecipherable games of the children while, at my side, a *guajiro* down from the sierra and a black guy dressed in pink and white, like a strawberry and lemon ice-cream, talk of Kennedy and Fidel, about dialectics and Marxism–Leninism.

The women flow down the centre of the street, twirling their parasols; the *guajiros* watch them from under the arcades in their straw sombreros, an obligatory cigar between the lips. A sign on the balcony of a housing-block reads:
LONG LIVE MARXISM.

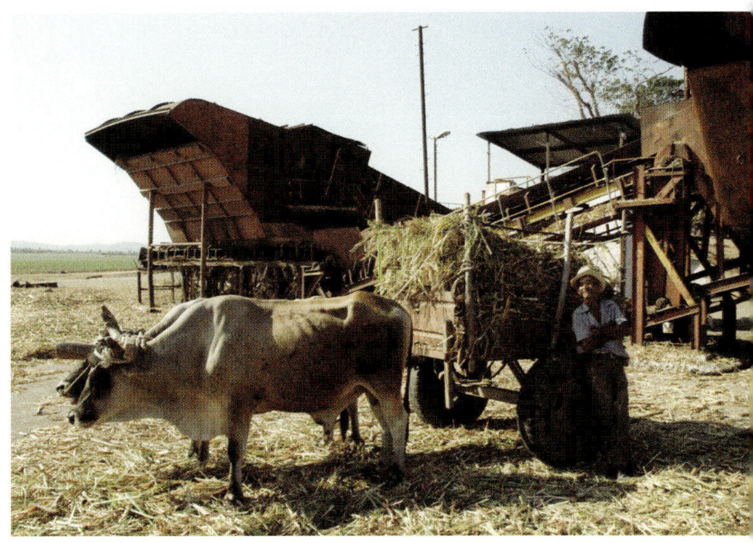

Soviet chaff-cutting machine, Holguín Province

12 APRIL. The Presidium of the Central Committee, the USSR's governing body, agrees to send the missiles and anti-aircraft guns requested by Castro the previous year. The month following, Khrushchev comes up with the idea of installing other missiles, with nuclear warheads, in Cuba. This is principally in response to the recent US deployment of medium-range Jupiter missiles in Italy and Turkey but, publicly, to safeguard Cuban sovereignty.

★

10 JUNE. Operation Anadyr, codename for the covert mission, is given the go-ahead by the Central Committee in Moscow. The plan is waved through despite warnings given by the engineers and officers sent on a recce to Cuba in the days previous. Namely, that palm trees provide insufficient cover from reconnaissance planes, so it may well be impossible to keep the mission secret. The largest of the missiles are twenty-five metres in length. They run on liquid fuel which requires lengthy pre-strike priming on large concrete launchpads, making them vulnerable to attack. Nevertheless, the manoeuvres are passed by the Commander of Strategic Missile Forces, Marshal Biriuzov, three days later.

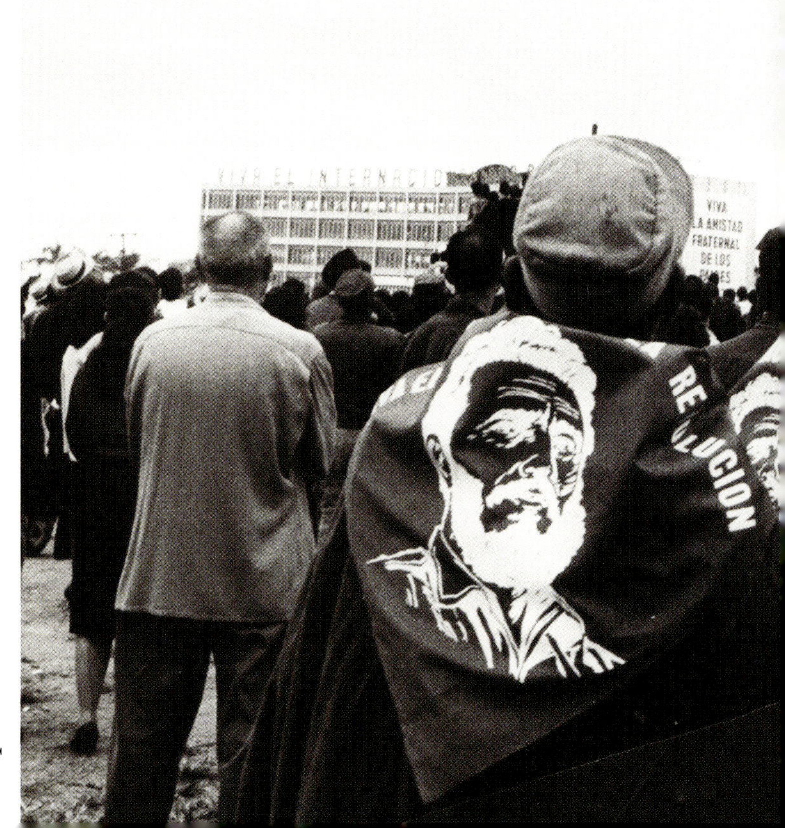

34

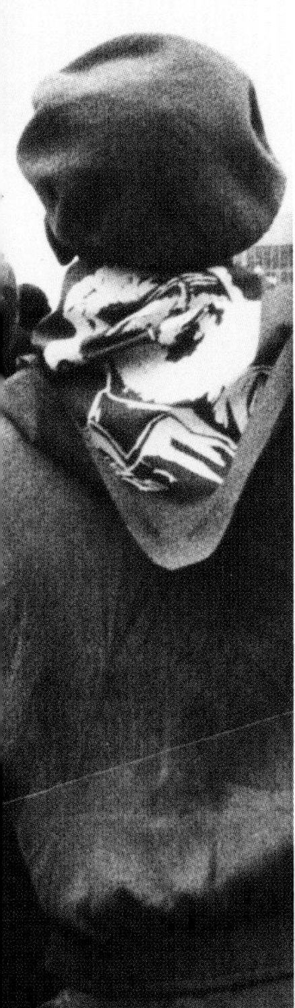

To defend the missile bases, forty-two MiG-21 fighter jets and extra consignments of surface-to-air missile batteries are to be sent to Cuba. Khrushchev invites a group of generals to the Kremlin from their missile base in present-day Ukraine, telling them they are going to 'shove a hedgehog' down Uncle Sam's pants. Raúl Castro, Fidel's brother, also in Moscow at this time to sign off the plan from the Cuban side, expressing concerns about how to keep the deployment secret, is reassured by Khrushchev with the claim he'll 'grab Kennedy by the balls' and force him to negotiate.

Sixty-year-old General Issa Pliev, a North Ossetian, is appointed the commander of the Group of Soviet Troops in Cuba, the official name of the task force. A former cavalry corps commander, in the Red Army and during the Second World War, he had fought on horseback alongside Soviet tank divisions following Stalingrad, making raids deep into German territory (his cruelty was such that even Stalin and Beria remarked on it). A man, then, with no knowledge of missiles; but the other members of the task force feel unable to voice their misgivings. Pliev is plagued by kidney problems, and is accompanied in Cuba by his own personal doctor.

JULY. Preparations begin for the transport of tens of thousands of Soviet officers, soldiers, and civilians. Eighty cargo ships are needed to carry the prefabricated concrete launchpads and missile hangars, forty missile launchers, sixty missiles with corresponding warheads. The troops called up to the ports for embarkation are given heavy winter clothes, lest anyone suspect the actual destination. Later, the rank and file are given coloured shirts – Operation Check Shirt is the nickname they give to the mission – and cloth caps; officers are distinguishable in pale shirts and hats. The generals, travelling mostly by plane, are given fake passports stating that they are 'agricultural advisors' or aeronautical engineers.

A second anti-aircraft unit, the Dnipropetrovsk Division, travels from Ukraine and is the first to arrive in Cuba in late July. (Eventually, eighty-five ships complete 150 round trips.) Within a week, rumours start circulating in the US about a Soviet military build-up on the island. These are dismissed by American intelligence services.

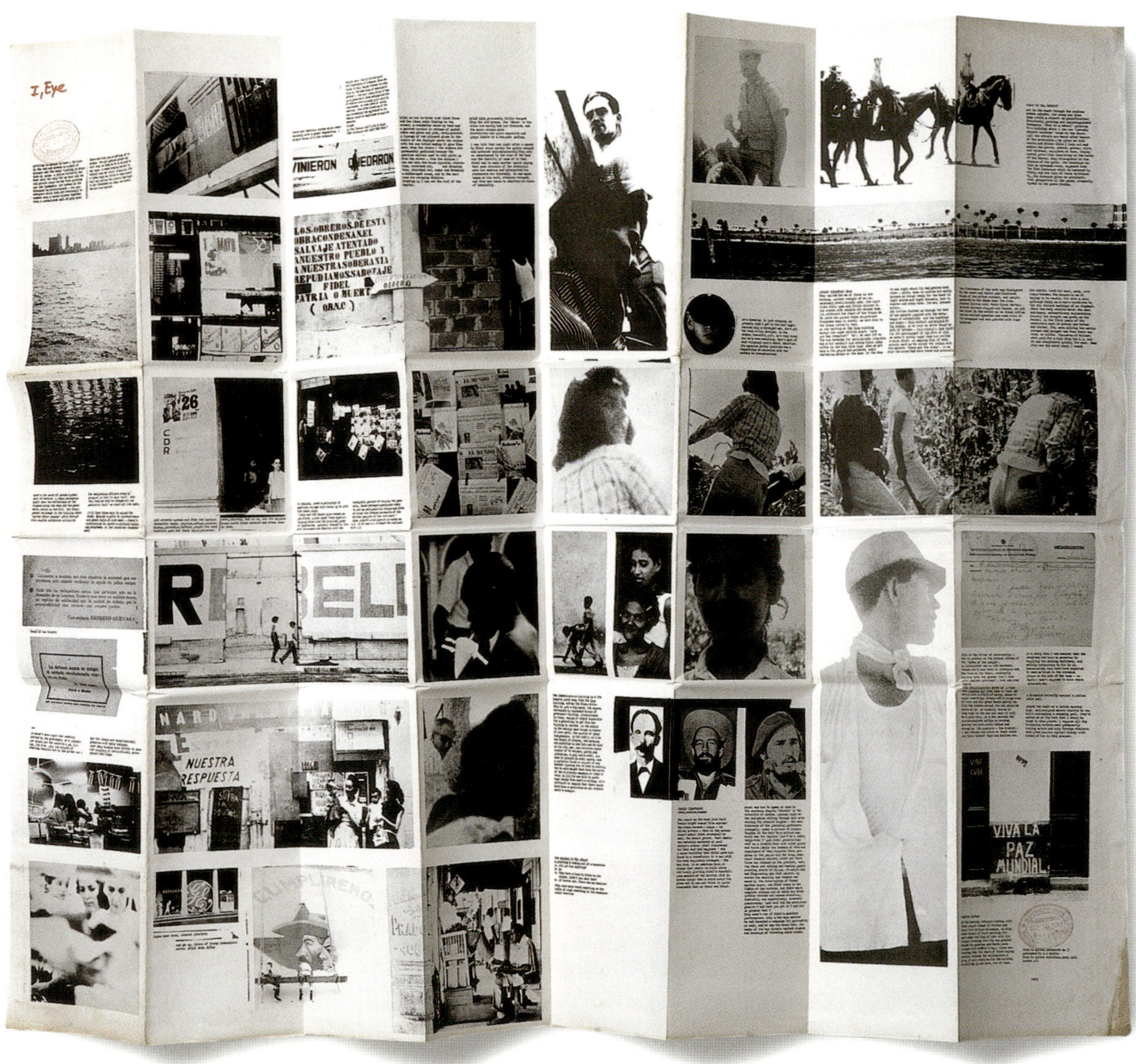

I,Eye **broadsheet**
published by Richard Hollis in London,
November 1962
Edited text and photographs begin
on the following pages

 4 AUGUST. **Leaving ancient Cadiz on the transatlantic crossing aboard the <u>SS Churruca</u>, a Spanish Line cargo vessel I'd joined in Barcelona. My first shipboard friendship: an old Jesuit, his hands like olive wood on the rail. Not Spanish, in fact, but Cuban – he left the country four years ago. The clasp fastening his waistbelt carries the words – in blue enamel, vivid against the black cassock – Colegio de Dolores: the school Fidel had gone to in Santiago de Cuba.**

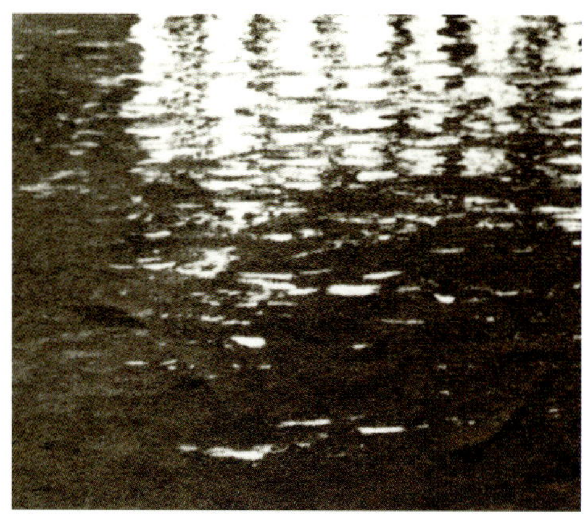

<u>Fellow travellers</u> (apolitically!)

① Colombian student of economics just finished tour of Europe writing for El Tiempo (Bogotá) slow discussions in French which haven't got very deep

② Dull philosophy student just finished 3 years at Salamanca University, as has ③ Young Jesuit cleric who is giving me Spanish lessons. He is really Cuban but left four years ago. He has "filled in the Cuba background" (Clem-like?) for me, but there's far too much to record about what he says. I gather that you are either a Fideliste or you aren't, and that soon there will be more who aren't than are.

Anyway, I find him most enormously impressive as a person. The only word which I can find for his quality is "efficient." He uses himself with people

---

I hope this letter isn't opened – just now I'm amazed by the complicated machinery of politics and trade. The ship stops for 3 days in Cuba to load and unload cargo, far longer than anywhere else. Unloading Spanish wire mesh for Fidel's new aerodromes (!) but most extraordinarily

 Colonel Ivan Sidorov sails from Sevastopol aboard the *Omsk*, a Japanese-built cargo ship. In the hold are hundreds of men and six R-12 missiles. For security reasons, the troops are not allowed above deck in daylight. Often, temperatures below reach 50ºC. (The hydrogen peroxide they carry, used to power the pumps of the rockets' combustion chambers, can become dangerously unstable above 35ºC.) When the deck hatches are thrown open, plumes of steam rise up.

Battened below, sweltering, the men spend their time watching and rewatching the patriotic epic *And Quiet Flows the Don*. KGB officers on board, running networks of informers helping them compile reports on morale among the troops, note that many have never been to sea before, most are seasick and upset about being denied statutory leave; there is widespread fear about how the US will react.

8 AUGUST. The *Ilia Mechnikov* sails from Odesa, passing through the Bosporus a week later under fake papers and accreditation. Even the ship's captain does not know his true destination, having been instructed to open a secret envelope only after successfully breaching the Strait of Gibraltar. When he does, nervously prising open the dossier on the bridge, the captain is confused to find a twenty-eight-page summary of the history of Cuba.

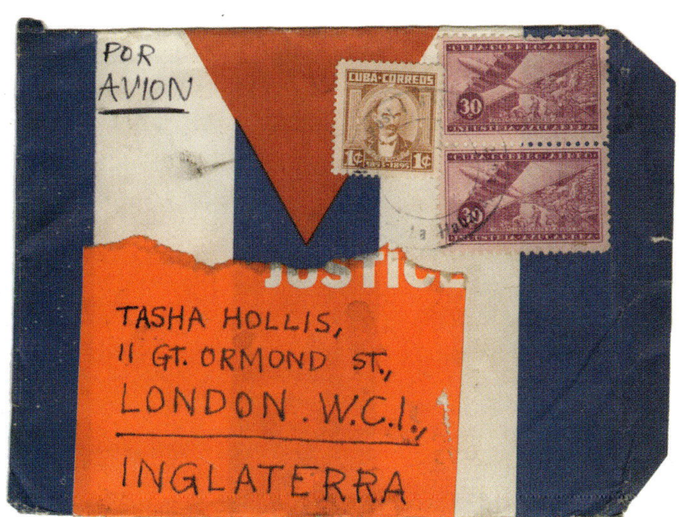

Dear Tasha,
While the priest may have failed to teach me Spanish, he's given me a thorough overview of the political situation. By his account, you are either a <u>Fidelista</u>, or you aren't — he'll remain in the former camp for as long as he's allowed to give communion. He talks of the food, even the women, of Cuba. And of Camilo Cienfuegos, the guerrilla leader who went missing in a plane crash during the first year of the Revolution.

The ship is full of rolls of wire fencing for Fidel's new aerodromes. Not quite Franco's willing contribution to the Revolution, you might imagine, but payment for being allowed to route Spanish exports to Czechoslovakia via Havana under a communist flag, I guess. (I suspect the priest of being some kind of spy.)
Love,
Richard

19 AUGUST. The first shipment of missiles – under the command of Colonel Sidorov – directed by mistake to the small south-coast port of Casilda, arrives. There is nowhere on the wharves to store them, so they remain aboard three weeks. The first medium-range R-12 missiles on Cuban soil – the second ever deployment of Soviet missiles outside the USSR – they are sent to El Purio, central Cuba.

The columns move only by night, the refrigerated missile lorries preceded by Cuban motorcyclists who close off the roads, staging traffic accidents (with elaborate theatre including the 'rescue' of wounded victims). Convoys contain five or six missile trailers and a protection unit. Decoy convoys are sent in directions opposed to the actual base sites. Occasionally, a building here and there has to be demolished to allow the long transports, with their twenty-five-metre-long missile trailers, to make turns.

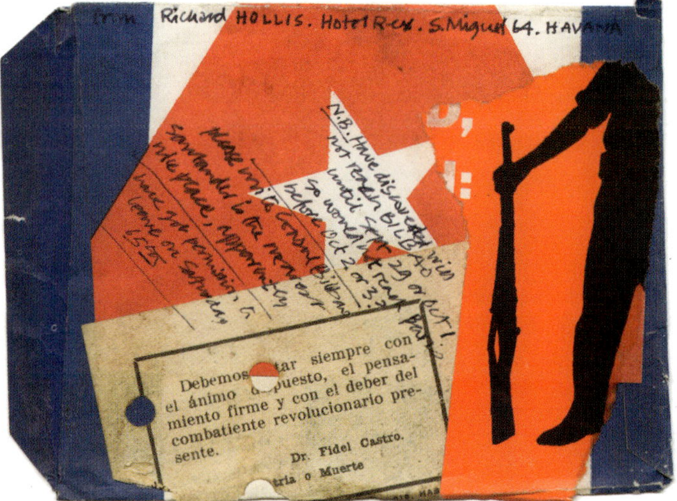

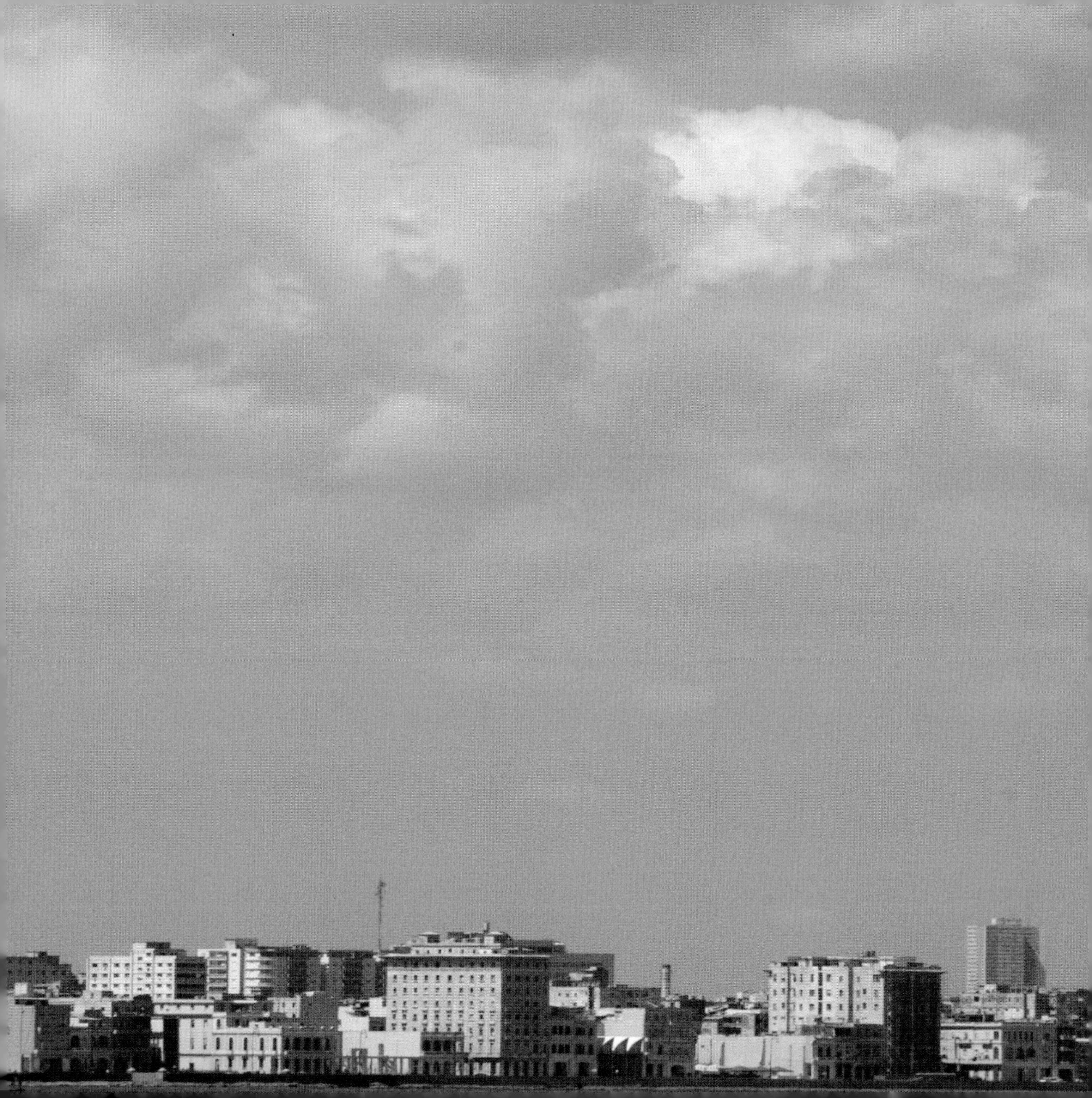

23 AUGUST. The approach to Havana. A yellow butterfly has been with the ship for an hour. Its repeated attempts at take-off, buffeted by thermals lifting off the Gulf Stream. Sweat trickles down my spine, pooling in the small of my back. A net of drizzle cannot obscure the extraordinary profile of the city. The priest points out to me the landmarks. A long, low, sweep of houses along the esplanade. The small cluster of modern sky-scrapers to the west. They huddle together in the grey mist.

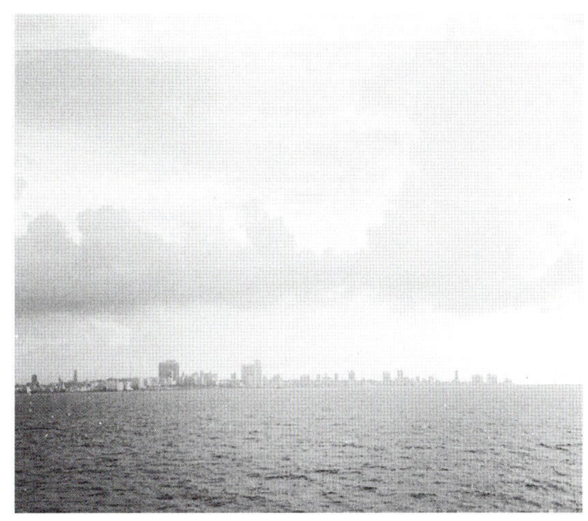

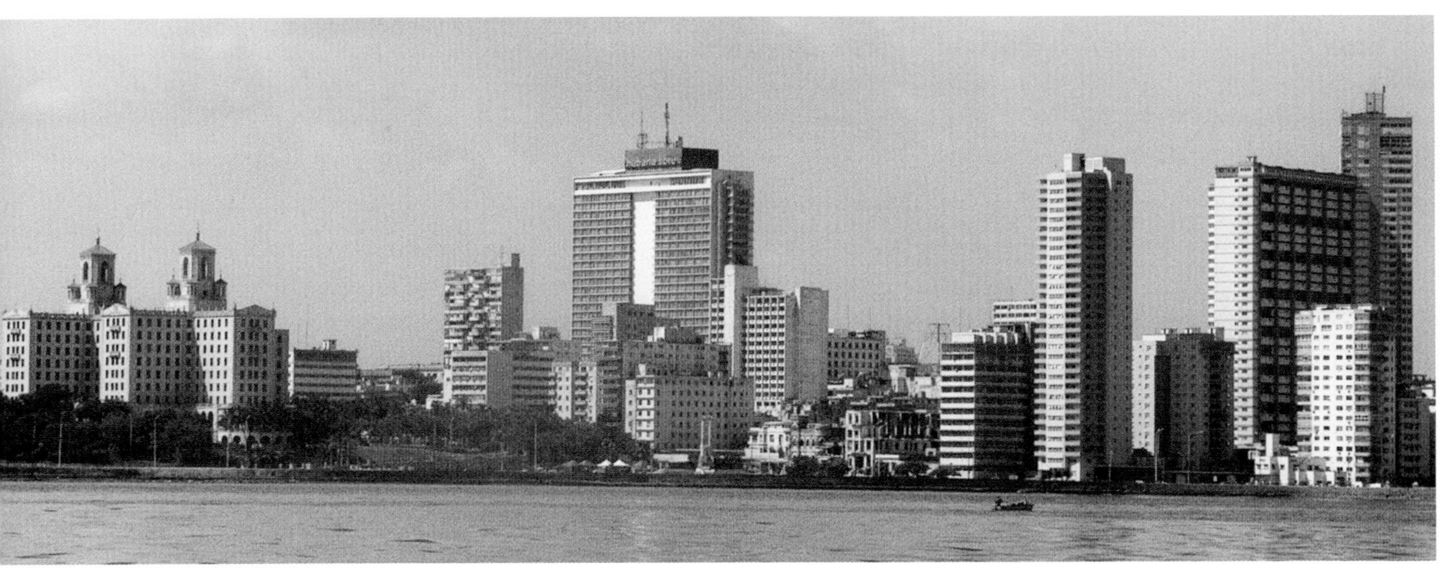

For the most part, Havana's architecture in the twentieth century aped foreign trends: the smart barrio of El Vedado became known as the 'American City'. The Modern Movement, begun partially in the 1940s, came to the fore in the 1950s along the rationalist lines of Le Corbusier, Gropius, Breuer and Mies. It was followed closely by Art Deco, Modern Monumental Movement, Organic Architecture and Brutalism. Construction, principally in El Vedado, tended towards a functional Modern aesthetic, an imposed individualistic style seen by some as a stifling influence on regionalist, home-grown trends. At the advent of the 1959 Revolution, Vedado's development – always underwritten by US dollars and often implemented by foreign architects or contractors – was such that, in the public imaginary, the barrio was associated with decadence, louche western cosmopolitanism, and the kind of hegemonic forces that the Revolution sought to topple. Even if it was, and remains, strategic as the highest point in Havana, it is symbolic that Castro commandeered the top storeys of the newly built Hilton – renamed the Habana Libre – as his command post after entering the city.

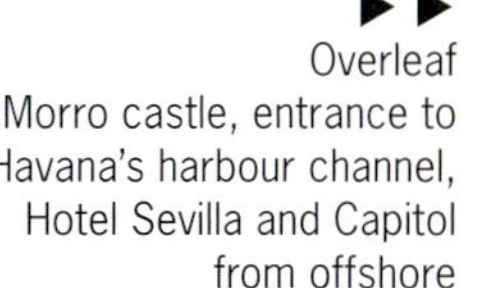

▶ ▶
Overleaf
El Morro castle, entrance to
Havana's harbour channel,
Hotel Sevilla and Capitol
from offshore

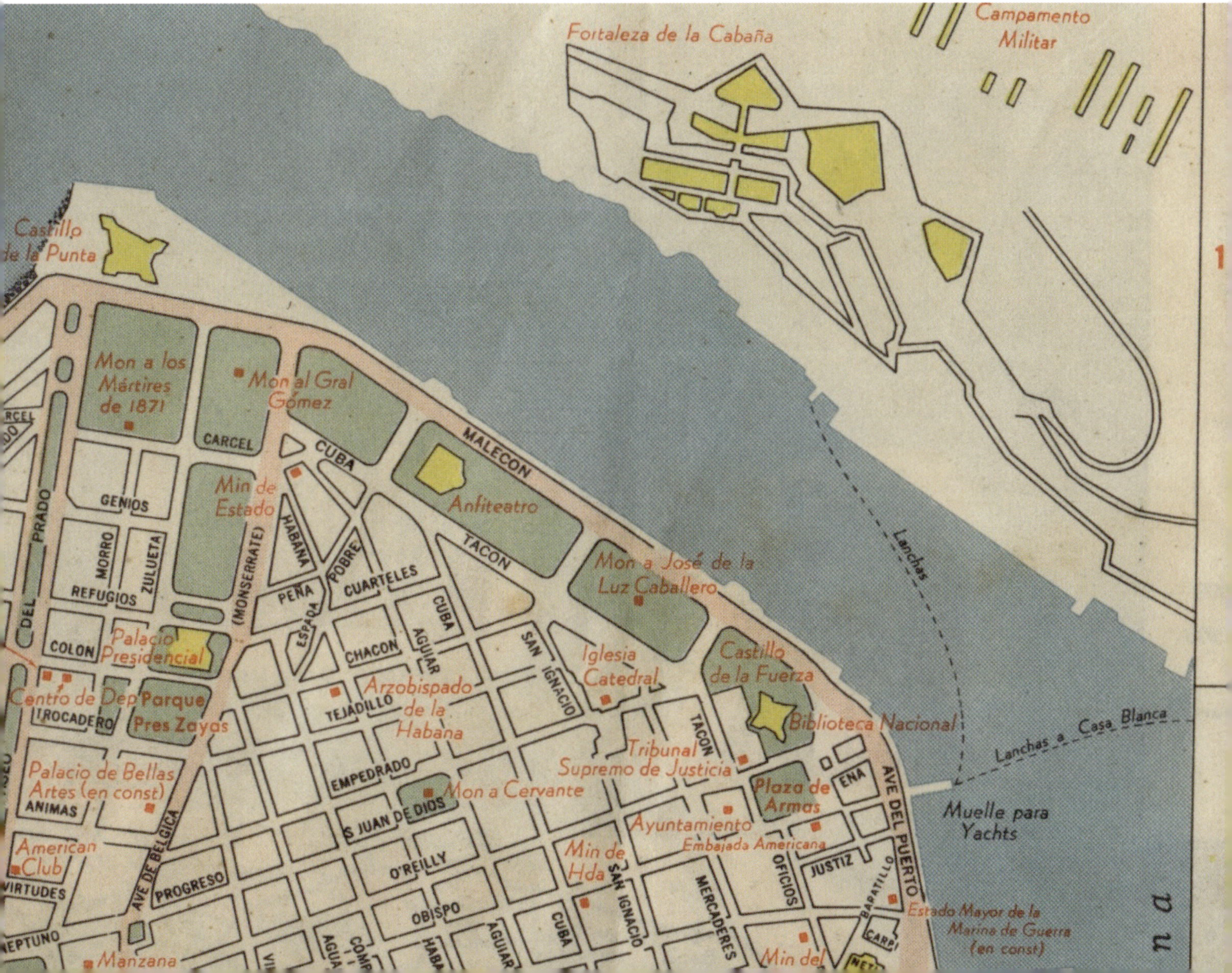

Fortaleza de la Cabaña
Campamento Militar
Castillo de la Punta
1
Mon a los Mártires de 1871
Mon al Gral Gómez
CARCEL
CUBA
MALECON
Min de Estado
Anfiteatro
GENIOS
(MONSERRATE)
HABANA
TACON
Mon a José de la Luz Caballero
MORRO
ZULUETA
PRADO
REFUGIOS
PEÑA
POBRE
CUARTELES
ESPADA
CUBA
AGUIAR
Lanchas
COLON
Palacio Presidencial
CHACON
SAN IGNACIO
Iglesia Catedral
Castillo de la Fuerza
Centro de Dep
Parque Pres Zayas
TROCADERO
TEJADILLO
Arzobispado de la Habana
Biblioteca Nacional
TACON
Lanchas a Casa Blanca
Palacio de Bellas Artes (en const)
EMPEDRADO
Mon a Cervante
Tribunal Supremo de Justicia
ANIMAS
ENA
AVE DEL PUERTO
Muelle para Yachts
American Club
S JUAN DE DIOS
Plaza de Armas
VIRTUDES
AVE DE BELGICA
PROGRESO
O'REILLY
Min de Hda
SAN IGNACIO
Ayuntamiento
Embajada Americana
MERCADERES
OFICIOS
JUSTIZ
BARATILLO
CARPI
NEPTUNO
Manzana
COMPO
AGUA
OBISPO
CUBA
HABA
AGUIAR
Min del
Estado Mayor de la Marina de Guerra (en const)
n a

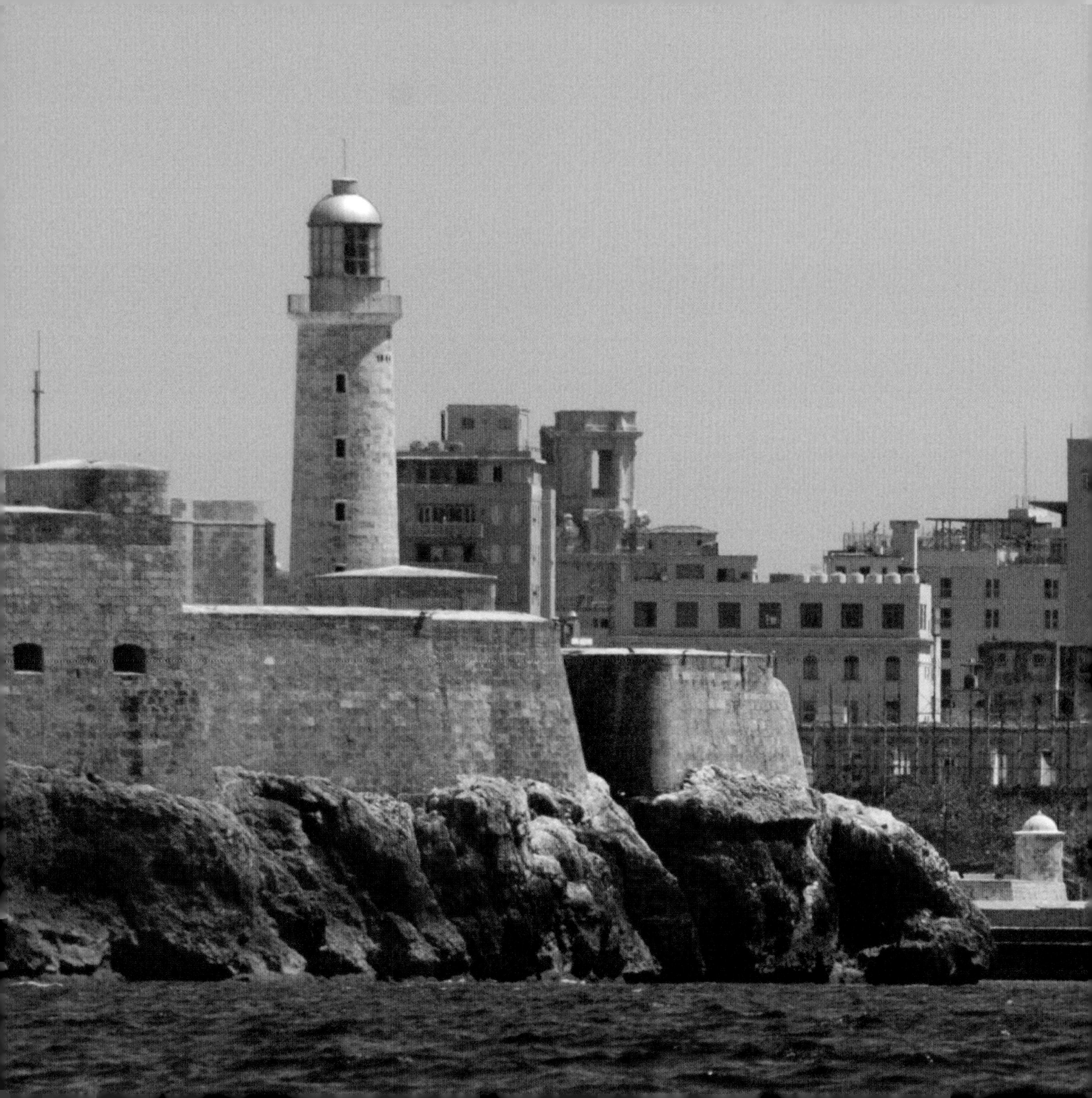

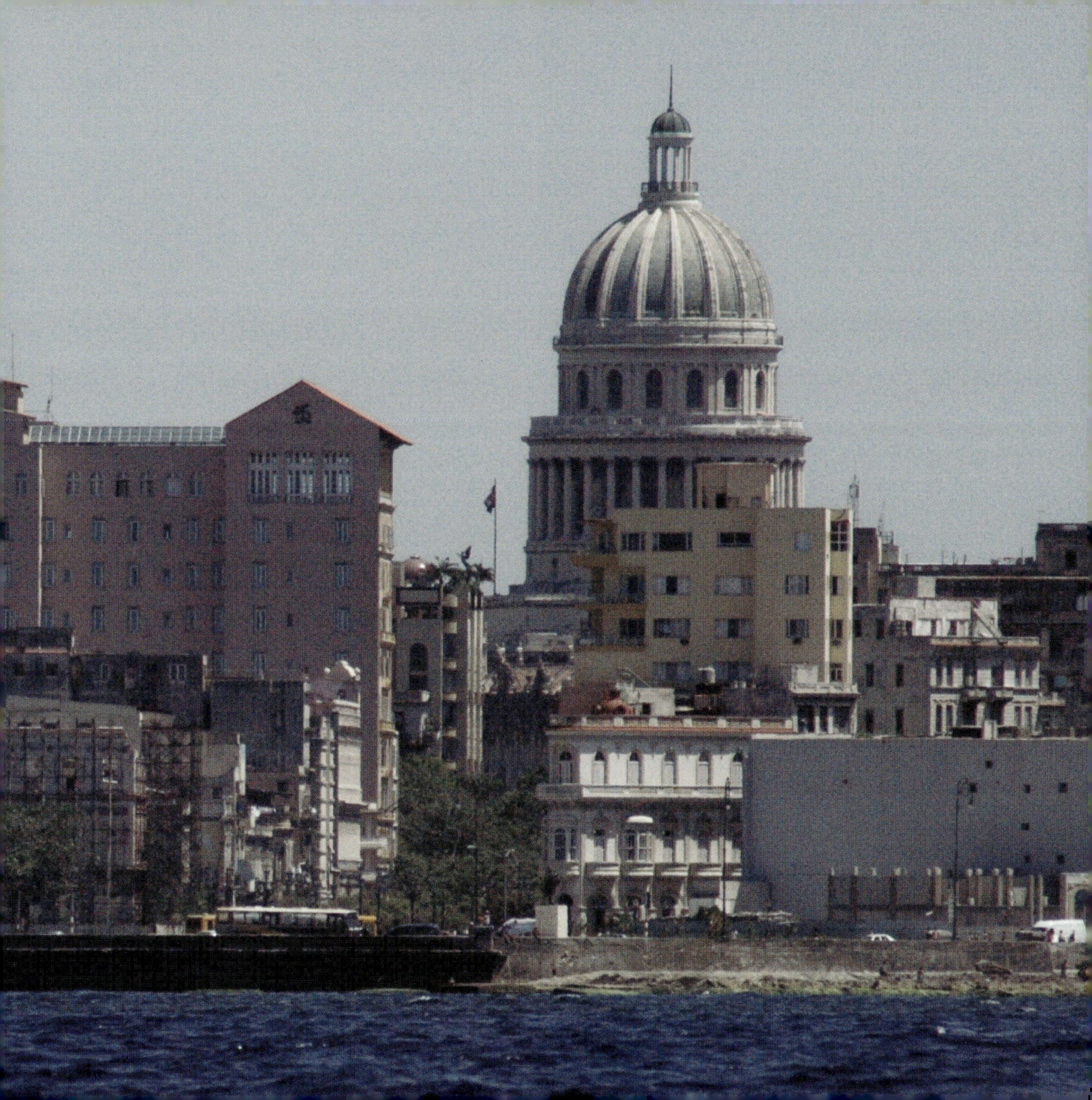

It is no accident that Sergio, the playboy protagonist of Tomás Gutiérrez Alea's classic film *Memories of Underdevelopment* (set in 1962), lords it over the city rooftops from his tastefully appointed apartment on the top floor of the FOCSA building, one of those high-rises adjacent to the former Hilton in Vedado. Sergio, cocooned as he is in a crow's nest papered with fashion mags and porcelain vases – stricken by an ennui burdened by his attentuated mode of living – peers down on a city peculiarly devoid (in his take on it) of human life in a view severely circumscribed by the telescope he cranes into. Camera shots with confined angles pan closely across walls: a microscopic diminution of a society in the throes of radical change.

This is a film which, in its incorporation of improvised scenes and direct sound, is the perfect – entirely Cuban – meeting of Soviet montage, Italian neorealism and early New Wave.

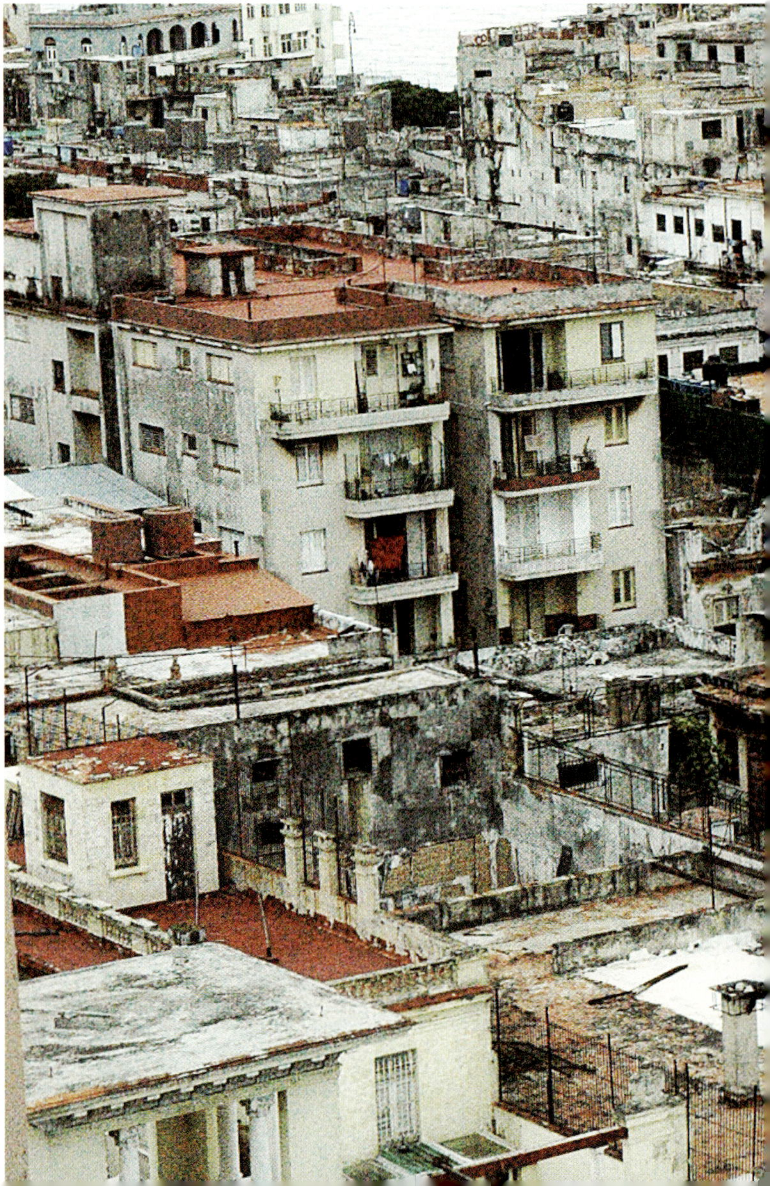

Everything carries on as before. Everything here is the same.
And all of a sudden it looks like a stage-set, a cardboard city.
Have I changed, or has the city changed?

— Sergio, *Memories of Underdevelopment*

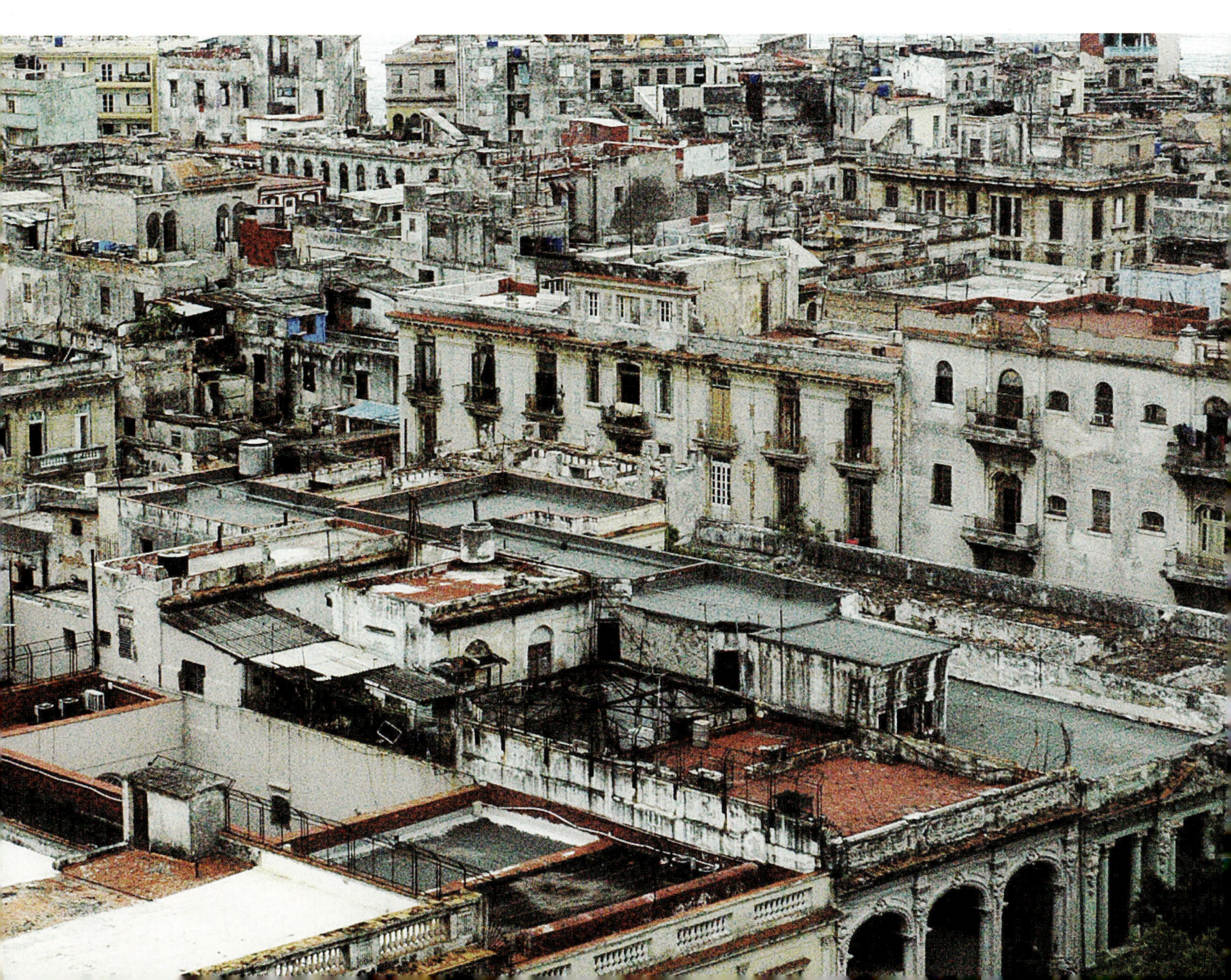

Memories of Underdevelopment:
Sergio wanders streets of Havana
passing CDR placard

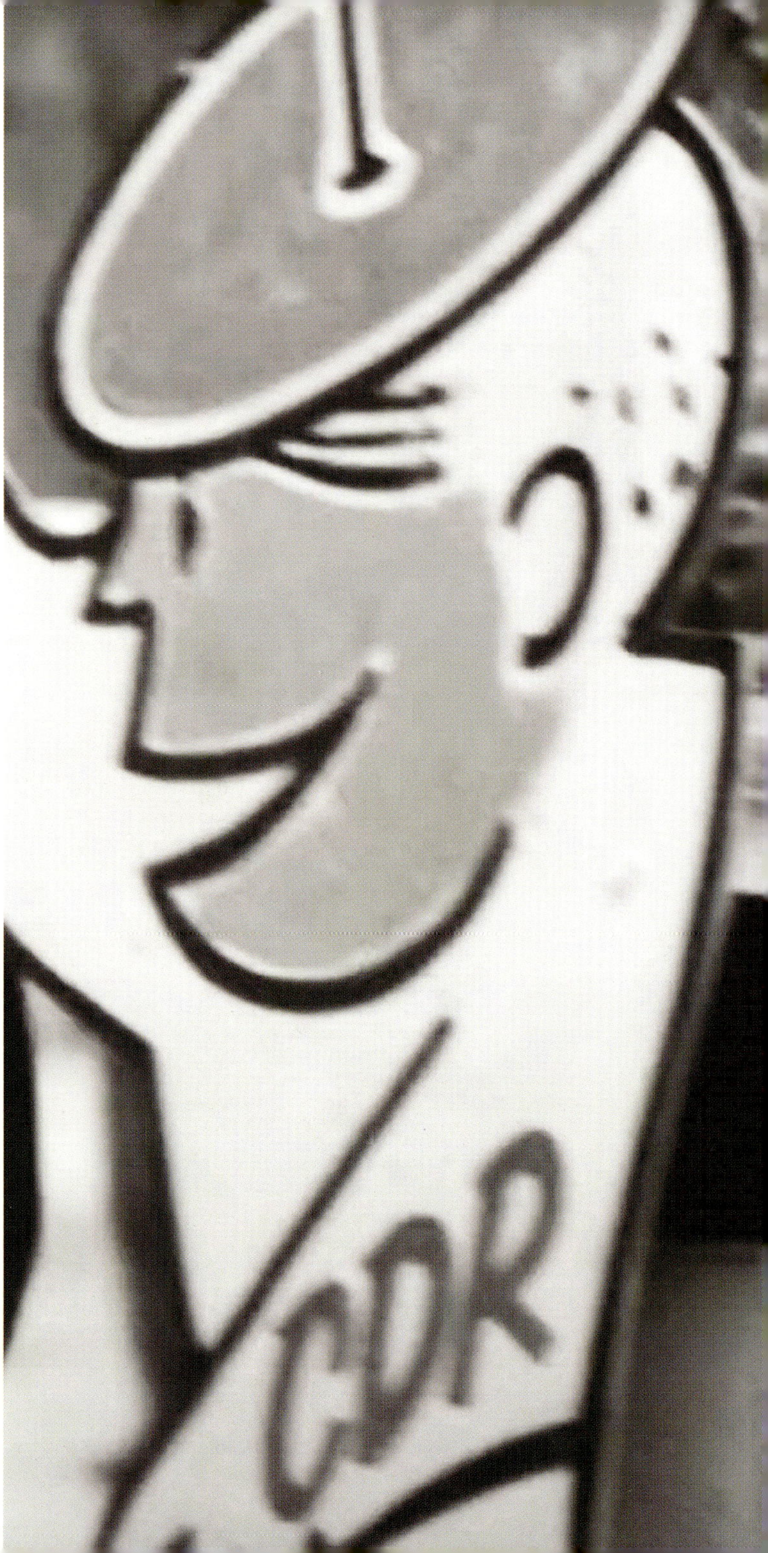

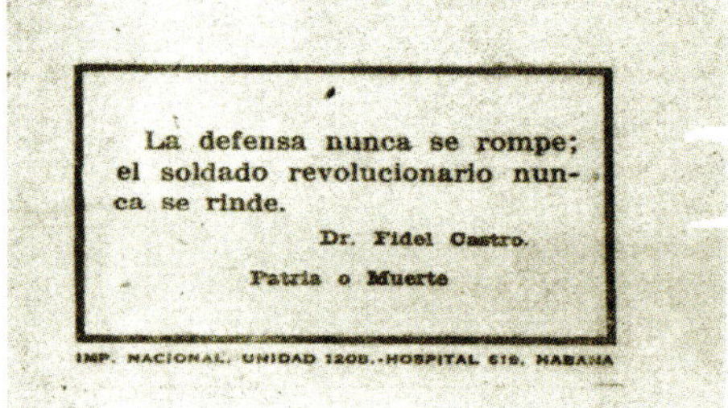

La defensa nunca se rompe;
el soldado revolucionario nunca se rinde.

Dr. Fidel Castro.

Patria o Muerte

IMP. NACIONAL. UNIDAD 120B.-HOSPITAL 619. HABANA

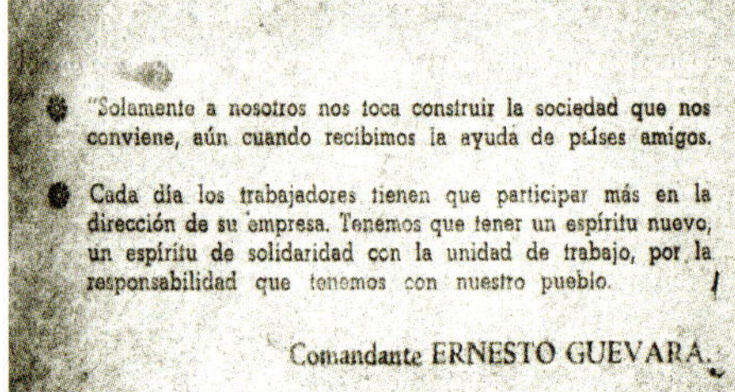

"Solamente a nosotros nos toca construir la sociedad que nos
conviene, aún cuando recibimos la ayuda de países amigos.

Cada día los trabajadores tienen que participar más en la
dirección de su empresa. Tenemos que tener un espíritu nuevo,
un espíritu de solidaridad con la unidad de trabajo, por la
responsabilidad que tenemos con nuestro pueblo.

Comandante ERNESTO GUEVARA.

Havana bus tickets:
exhortations from Dr Fidel Castro
and comandante Che Guevara

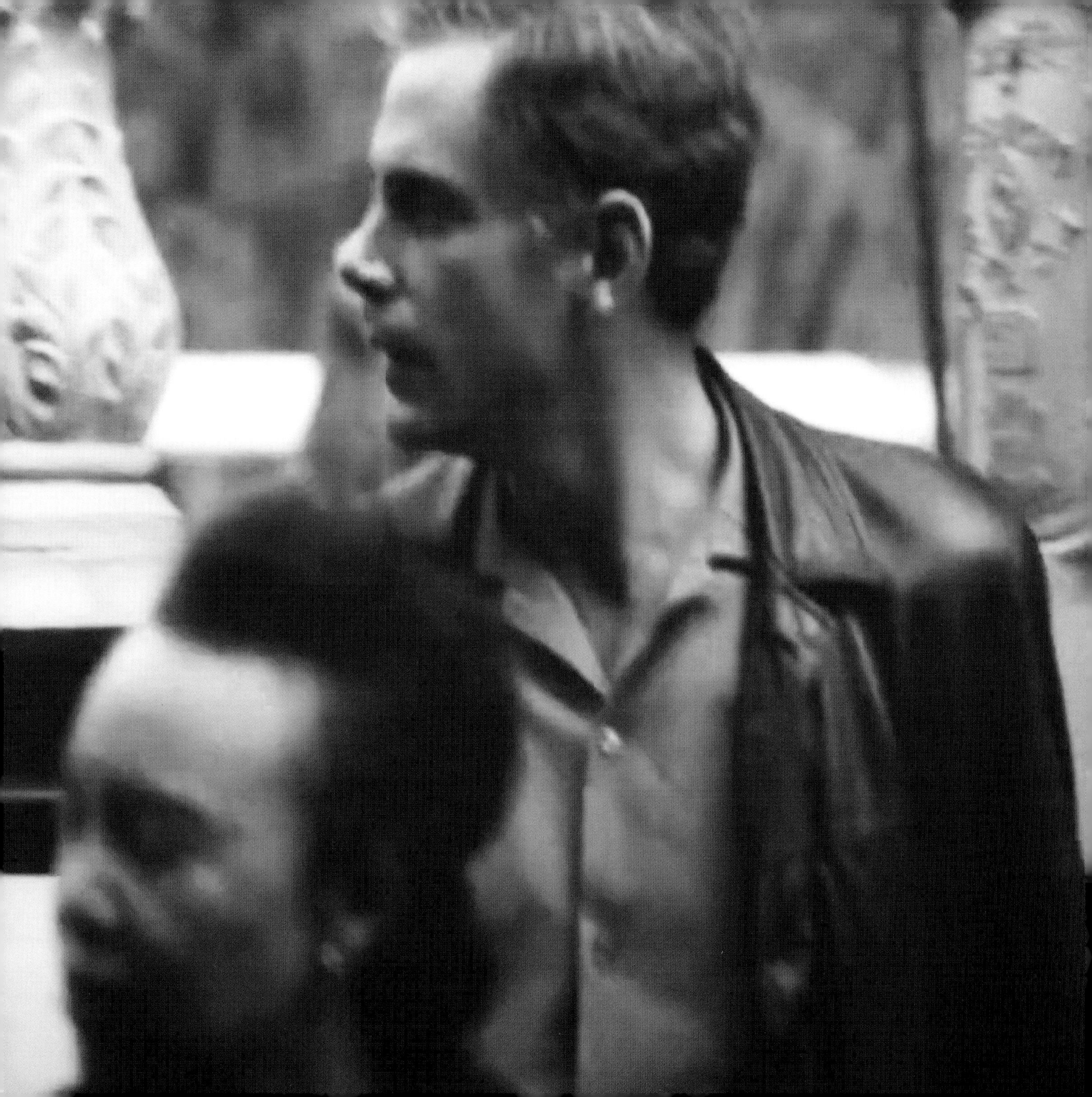

The maze-like Old Town nested
alongside the harbour, diamond-
shaped and full of mystery. I'm at
the Hotel Rex, Centro Havana.
Streets with marvellous names
stretch out like spokes from a
hub: Sun, Light, Neptune, Loyalty,
Refuge, Concord, Bishop,
Salvation, Friendship, Virtues
(denizen of less-than-virtuous
trade).

Terrific storms that unfold with a
giant thunderclap, like the report
from a gun. Talk of invasion is on
everyone's lips. What will be the
pretext? A plane, marked up in
Cuban colours, attacks the US
naval base at Guantánamo. Or a
Cuban expeditionary force, in fact
led by exiles, attacks a
neighbouring Central American
country. An action roundly
condemned in the halls of the
Organisation of American States.
Lettered on a wall, a question:

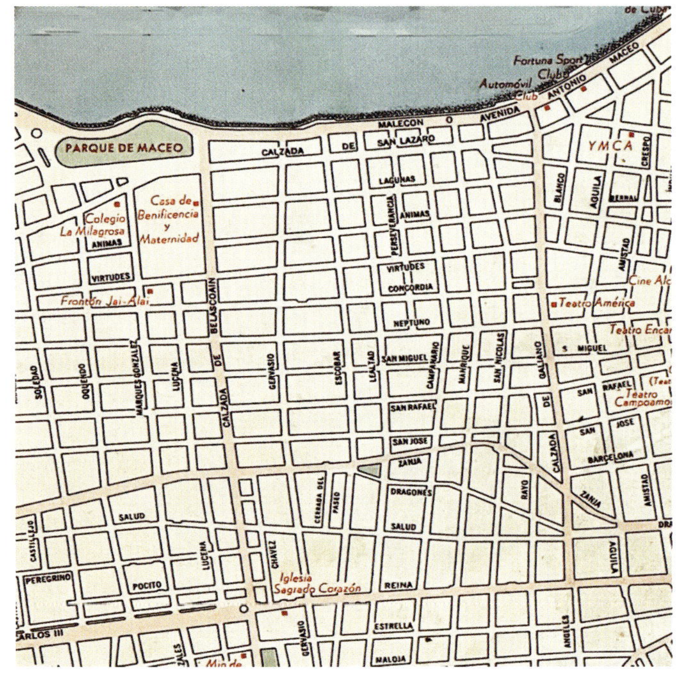

IF THE YANKEES CAN'T LIVE 90
MILES FROM SOCIALISM, WHY DON'T
THEY MOVE AWAY ?

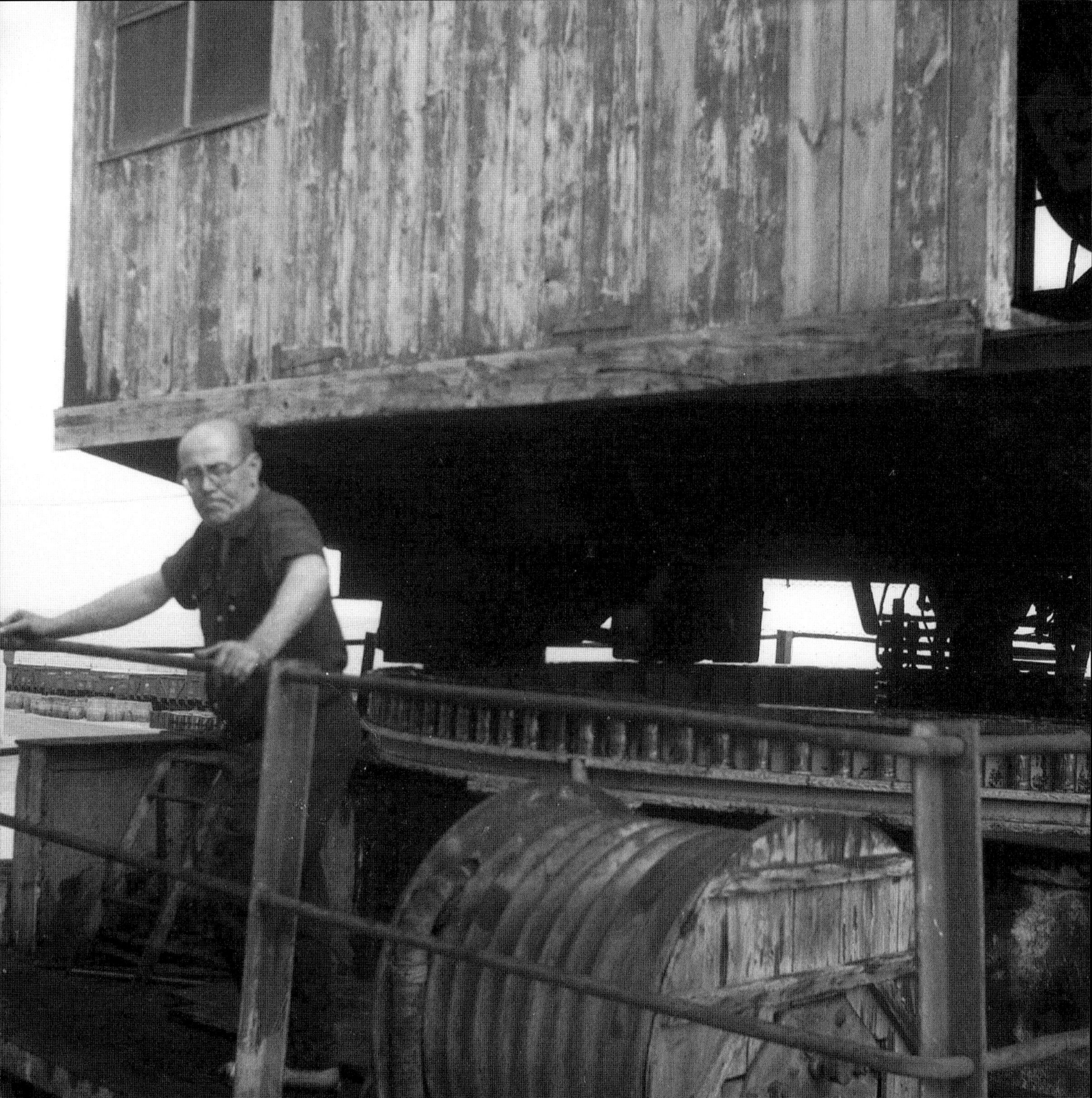

22 AUGUST. It is taking an age to unload the cargo. Much longer than in Tenerife, San Juan, Port-au-Prince. Just a handful of us disembarking. The Jesuit. The musician (in need of medical attention). A quiet woman with a small child kept to herself the whole way. Me, the optimistic British tourist. Now, the still, flat expanse of Havana's great harbour.

The great white Christ above the harbour channel, a hand raised in benediction. Revolutionary slogans reflected in the water, the former logo of the United Fruit Company still visible under the whitewash of VIVA NUESTRA REVOLUCIÓN SOCIALISTA. The immigration officer stamps EXIT on our passports. Realising the mistake, the whole process starts again.

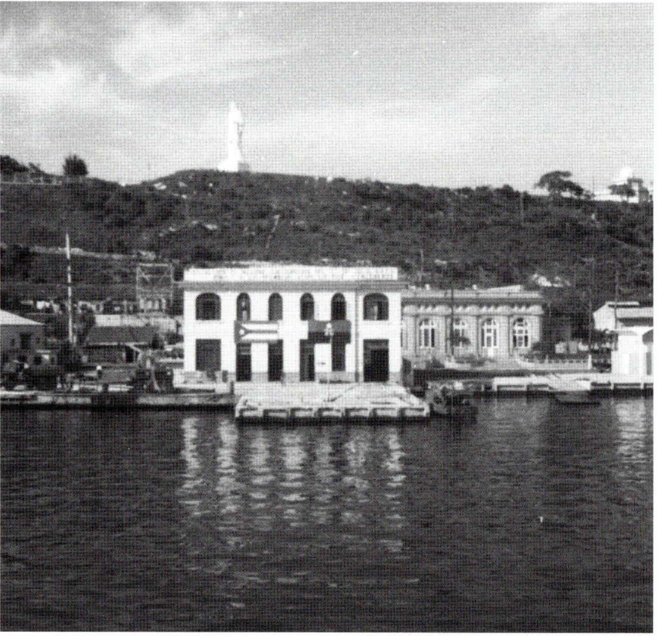

25 AUGUST. US intelligence identifies the presence of Soviet MiG-21 fighter jets in Cuba, and several new surface-to-air missile sites which are deemed defensive in nature, having a range only of twenty miles.

Tony Évora shows me some of the nightlife, not so different to that of the old Havana. 'Shows' in all the clubs: mostly bad, frenzied; the music is always good. Over white label rum, he talks to me of typefaces, Henryk Tomaszewski, Lubalin, El Lissitzky, De Stijl, Push Pin Studios, and Schwitters.Tony designs Lunes the Monday cultural supplement to Revolución newspaper and for its book publishing offshoot.

In Bohemia magazine, under a photograph of American boys lining up to join the Peace Corps: 'These are Yankee spies masked as pacifists. Hidden under those angelic-looking faces lies the homicidal power of imperialism. Specially trained to live among Latin American families with the deceitful pretext of helping the peasants, these Pentagon agents are ready to act as anti-guerrilla troops and drench in blood the liberation movements of our continental brethren.' Cuban counter-intelligence is known as the G2. If it were the G1, it might be confused with 'GI'.

Pimps, still ubiquitous, risk ten years in jail: the girls have raised their prices due to the increasingly precarious life.

I'm told that, one night directly following a speech by Fidel on the theme of 'public morals', the police swooped and arrested indiscriminately. Such was the size of the haul and identity of some of those detained, the commander-in-chief had quickly to issue a clarifying statement: some elements of the Revolution tend towards over-zealousness, and that his own pronouncements should not always be taken at their word. Everyone was released. The leader's statement immediately taken as a green light.

Camilo Cienfuegos. Most genuinely
popular of all the guerrilla
commanders. Definitely murdered on
Raúl Castro's orders, the priest
told me. Fidel discovered too
late what had happened. A nurse
testifies that Fidel gave his blood
in a transfusion to a man with his
head completely bandaged. The man
died. An American book claims that
Camilo is still alive, busily
plotting Fidel's downfall. But
even members of the British Club
in Havana accept that a storm
swept his plane out to sea, and
think it quite reasonable that no
trace was found.

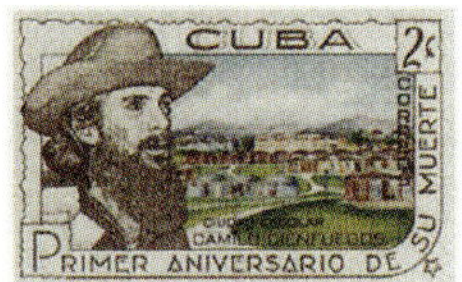

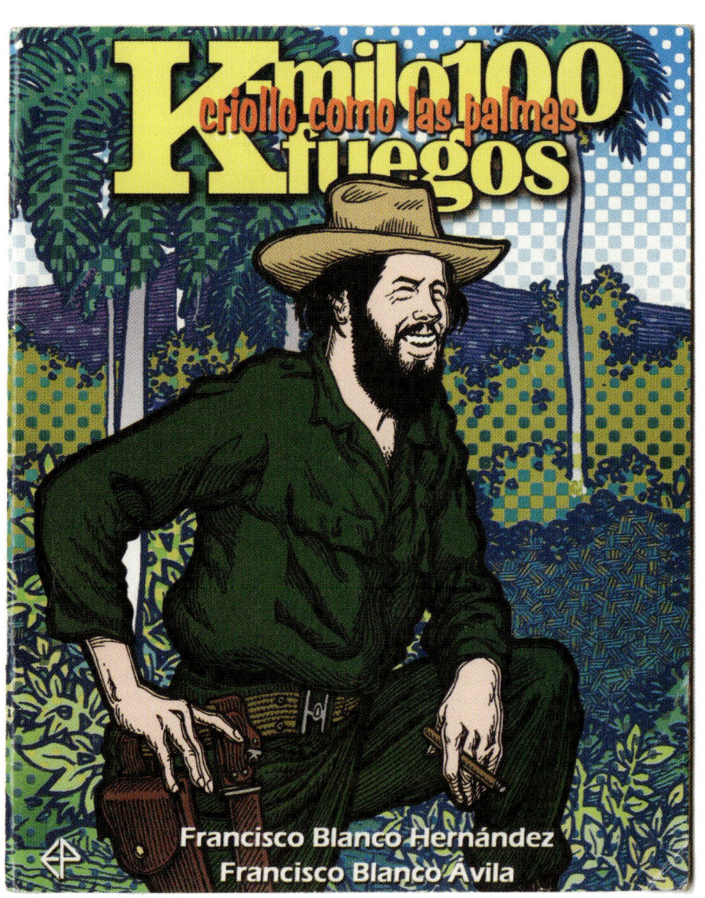

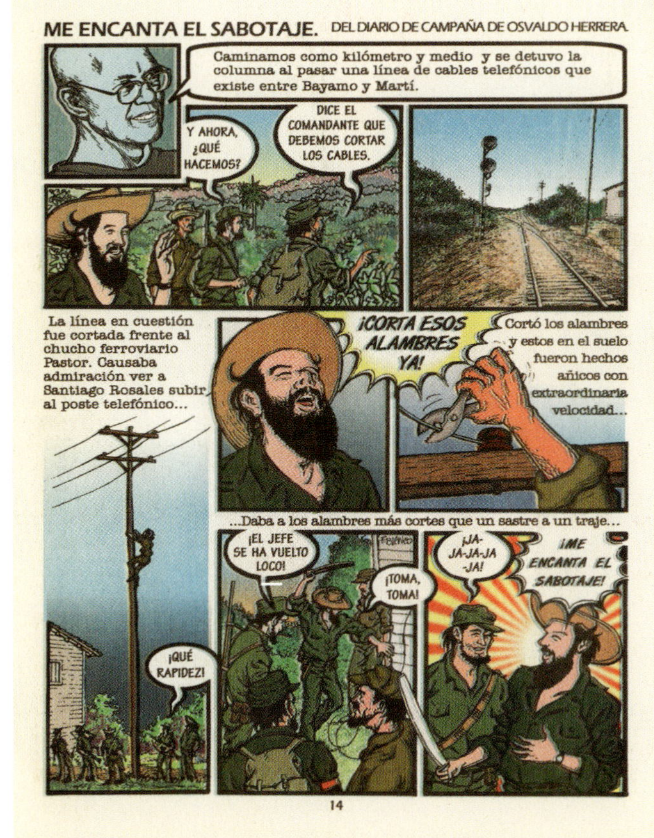
ME ENCANTA EL SABOTAJE. DEL DIARIO DE CAMPAÑA DE OSVALDO HERRERA.
Caminamos como kilómetro y medio y se detuvo la columna al pasar una línea de cables telefónicos que existe entre Bayamo y Martí.
Y AHORA, ¿QUÉ HACEMOS?
DICE EL COMANDANTE QUE DEBEMOS CORTAR LOS CABLES.
La línea en cuestión fue cortada frente al chucho ferroviario Pastor. Causaba admiración ver a Santiago Rosales subir al poste telefónico...
¡CORTA ESOS ALAMBRES YA!
Cortó los alambres y estos en el suelo fueron hechos añicos con extraordinaria velocidad...
...Daba a los alambres más cortes que un sastre a un traje...
¡EL JEFE SE HA VUELTO LOCO!
¡TOMA, TOMA!
¡JA-JA-JA -JA!
¡ME ENCANTA EL SABOTAJE!
¡QUÉ RAPIDEZ!
14

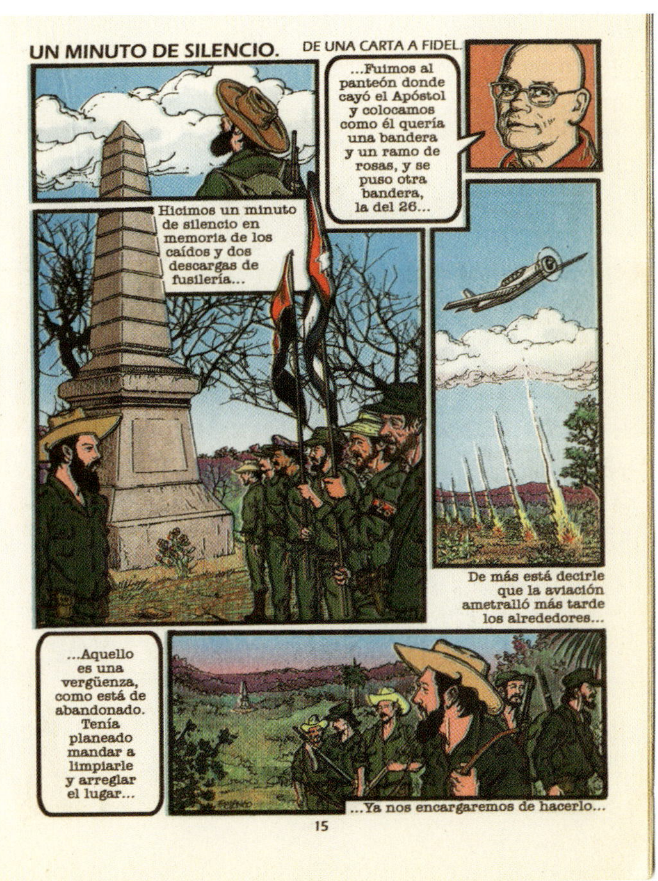
UN MINUTO DE SILENCIO. DE UNA CARTA A FIDEL.
...Fuimos al panteón donde cayó el Apóstol y colocamos como él quería una bandera y un ramo de rosas, y se puso otra bandera, la del 26...
Hicimos un minuto de silencio en memoria de los caídos y dos descargas de fusilería...
De más está decirle que la aviación ametralló más tarde los alrededores...
...Aquello es una vergüenza, como está de abandonado. Tenía planeado mandar a limpiarle y arreglar el lugar...
...Ya nos encargaremos de hacerlo...
15

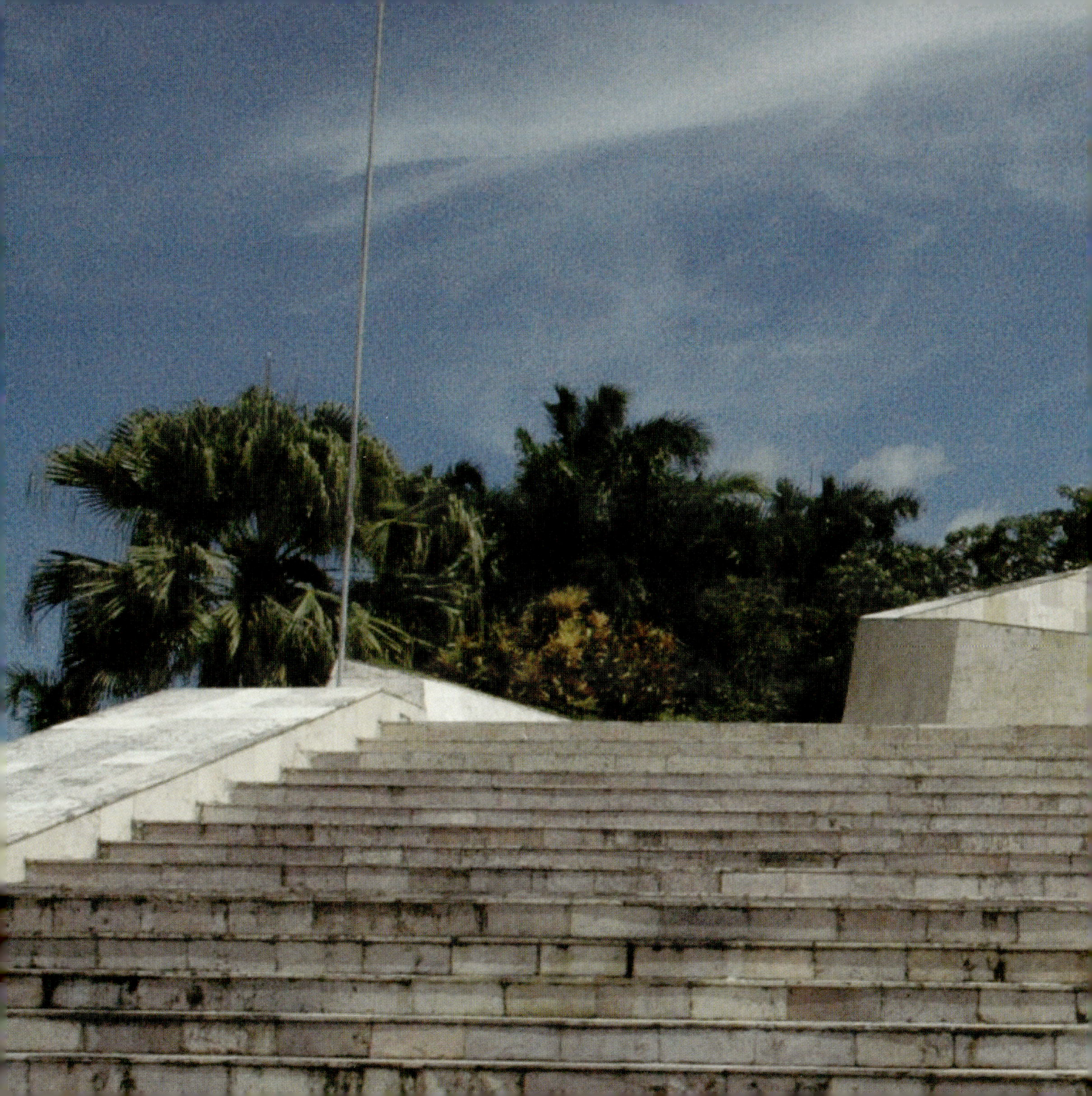

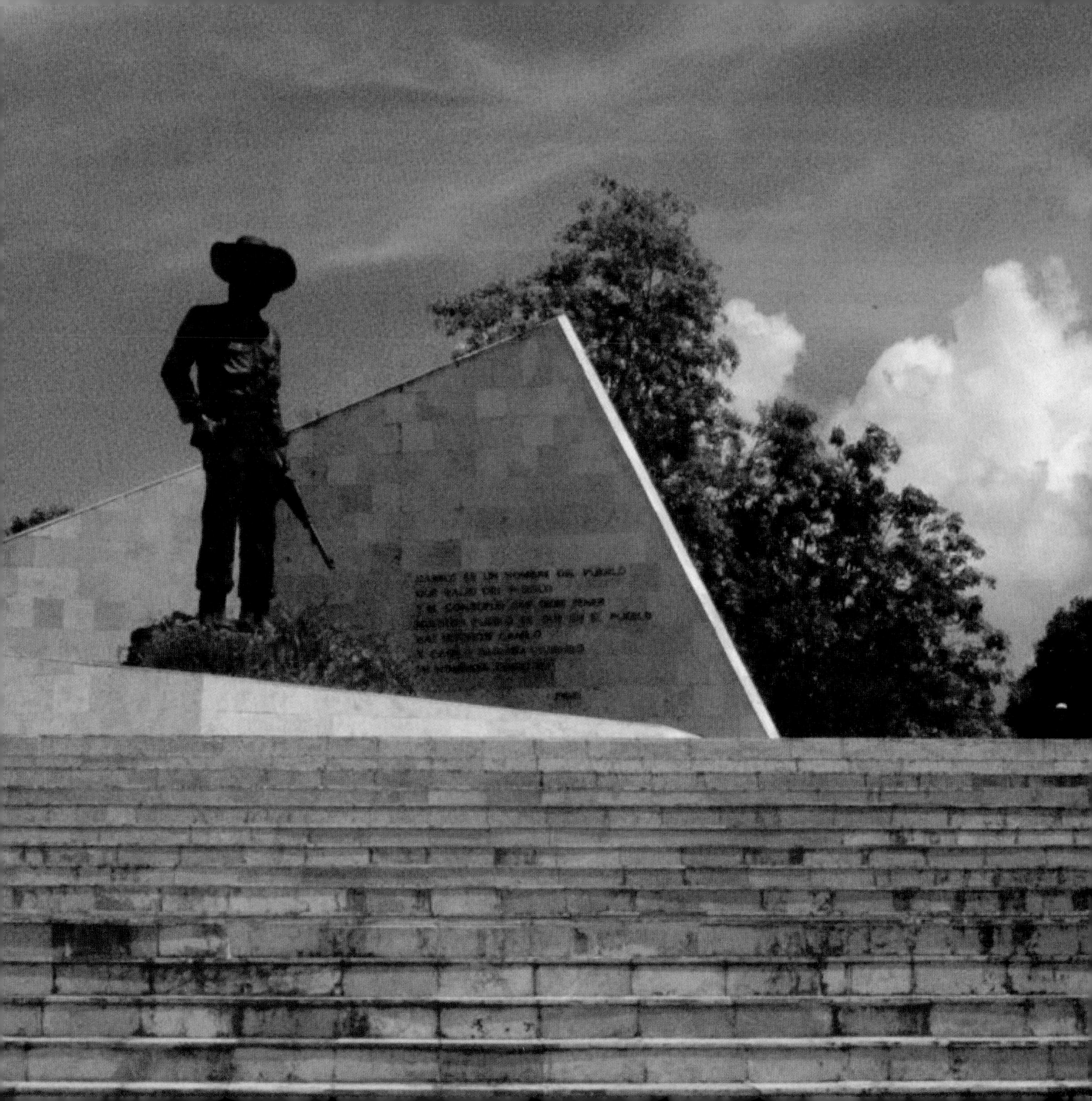

José Testón, Santa Cruz de Los Pinos, western Cuba. In July '62 the farm which he now runs is selected by a Soviet technician for use as a covert missile base. Soon, it becomes home to a regiment of eight thousand officers and soldiers, guarding thirty-six R-12 missiles. Their commander is Major General Igor Statsenko, a native of Chornobyl in Ukraine. Part of the agreement between the two governments is that the missiles are to remain entirely under Soviet control. No Cubans, even the military, are allowed inside the base, guarding instead the perimeter. But Testón states that the Soviets would sneak out now and again, to chase the local women and procure a kind of 90%-proof rum Cubans use only as disinfectant. He recalls hearing of US spy planes swooping over his farm.

These were Crusaders flown by the US Marine Corps out of Key West, Florida, flying at one thousand feet over their targets, photographing four frames a second, or one shot every seventy yards, providing evidence that was later displayed at the United Nations. (Spy planes conducted their overflights at 72,000 feet.) Statsenko, the base commander and a lover of poetry, is a decorated veteran of the Second World War. At forty-three he has just been elevated to the rank of general and commands the four regiments of the 43rd Missile Division. It was a matter of national pride that his R-12s, based in Okhtyrka, could reach Vienna; his R-14s, from their launch sites in Lebedyn and Hlukhiv, could reach Paris.

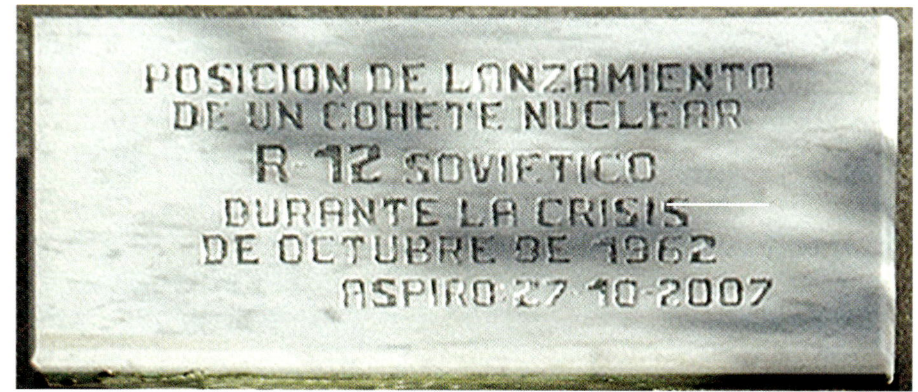

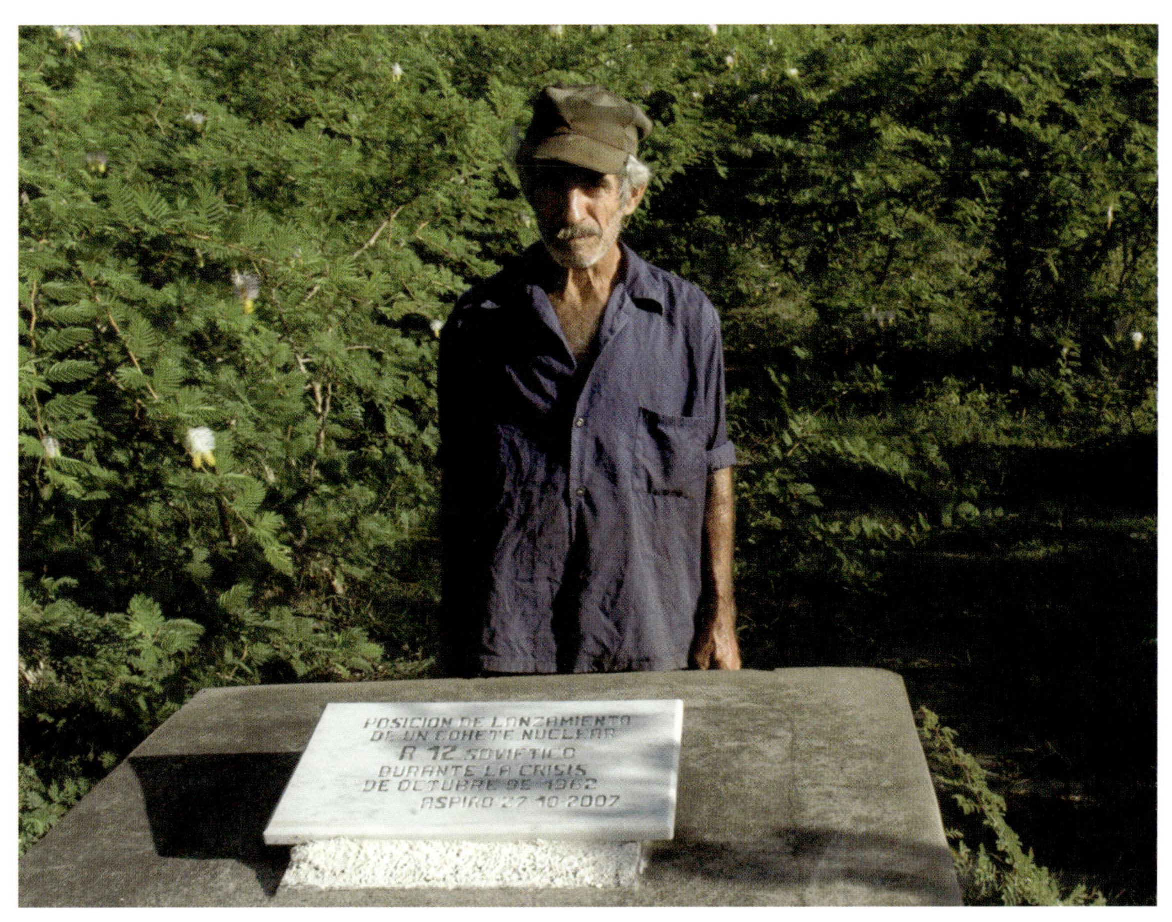

José Testón, farmer of the land
at former missile launch site,
Santa Cruz de Los Pinos

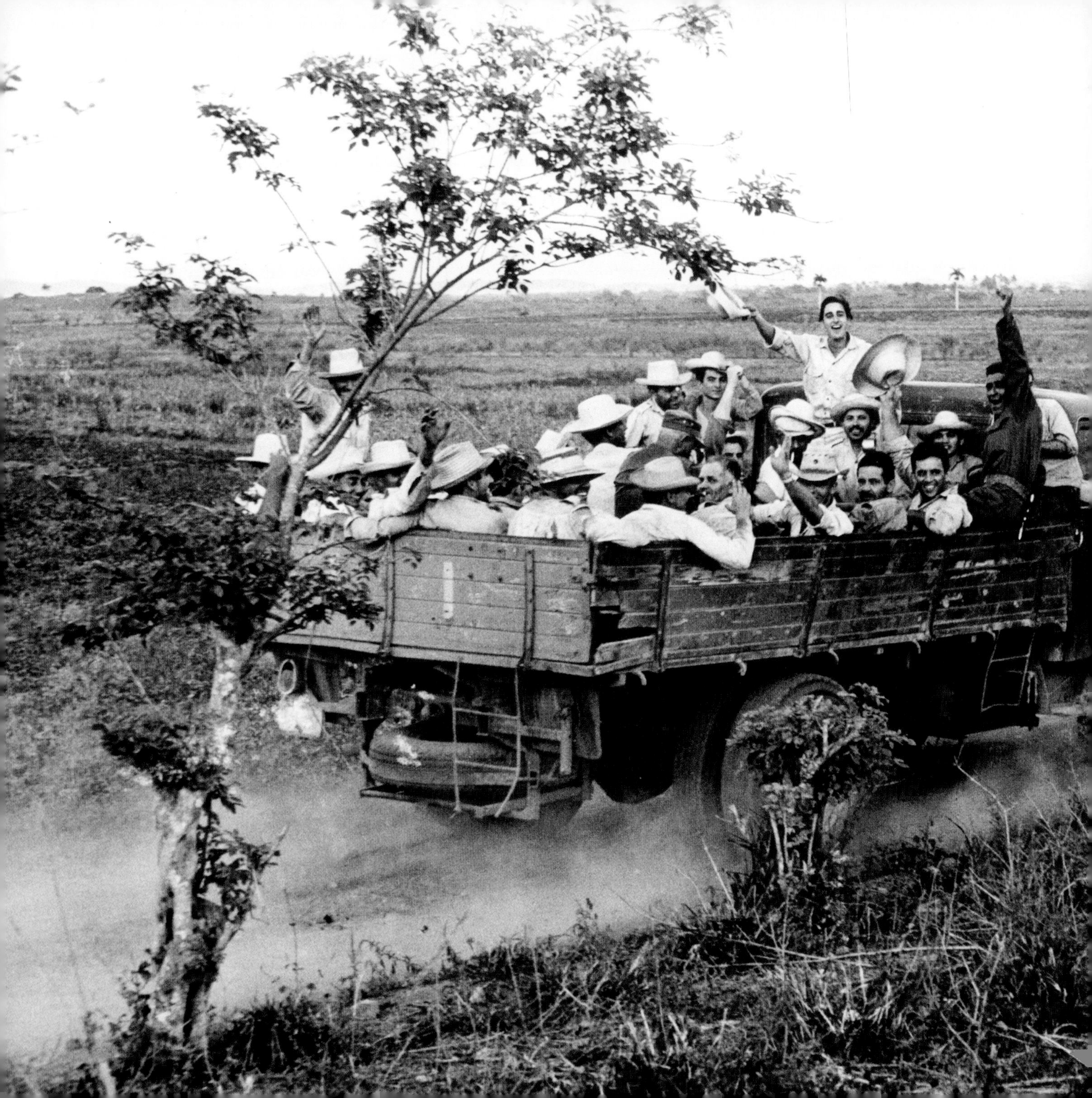

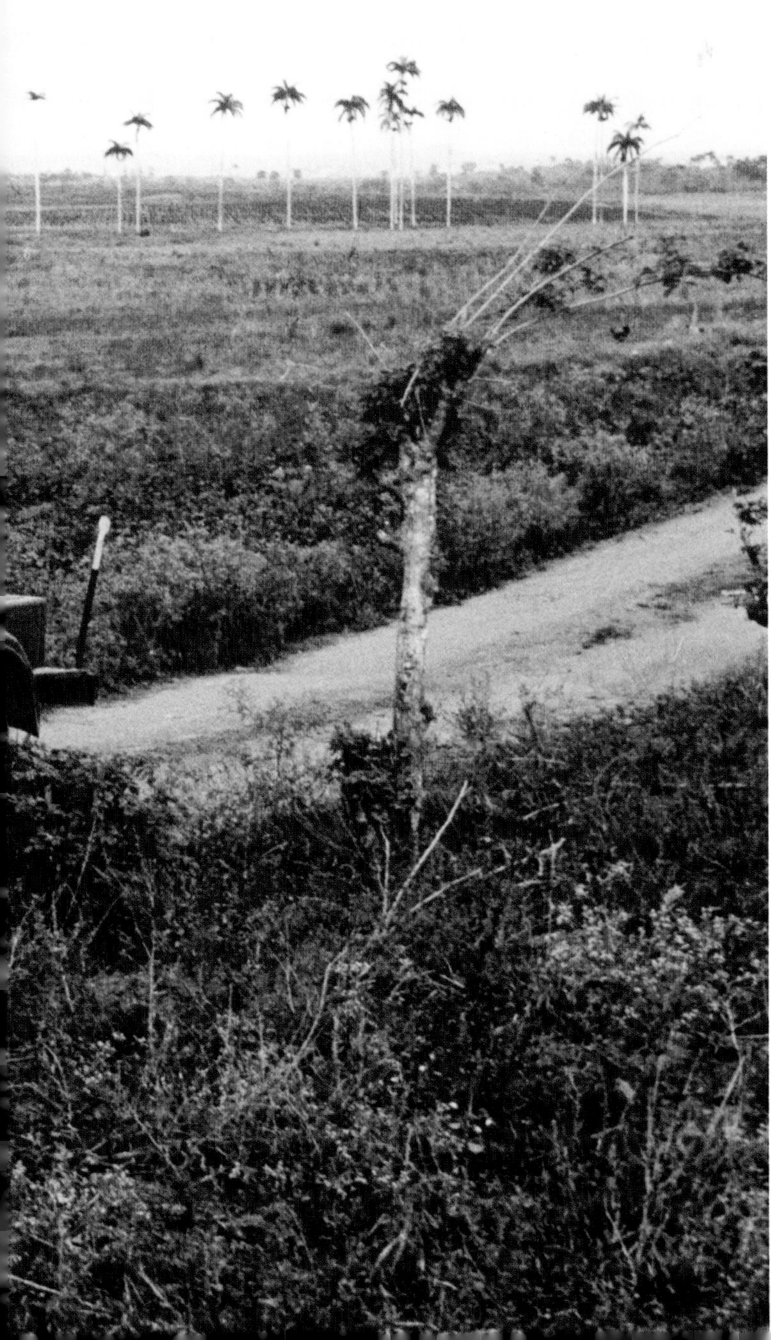

Off to work in the fields
photo © Luc Chessex

Sunday voluntary work. They call for me at 3am. Clear example of gratuitous revolutionary zeal. Nightclubs still open.Little shrines in the street with candles lit around them (in honour of the feast of the Virgin of El Cobre, who guided three shipwrecked fishermen to the shore). We go down to the Plaza Cívica by taxi. No one's waiting at the INRA building (National Institute for Agrarian Reform) except of course a militiaman. 'Have you had breakfast?' 'No.' We go off to the bus station for (nationalised) Coca-Cola, a hot sandwich and strong black Cuban coffee in the standard tiny blue cups. Back at the INRA, a few people are now gathered, small chattering group in the dark. By the time it's light, about a hundred and fifty have greeted each other – girls, some in uniform, but mostly dressed as though ready for the beach in light shirts and tight trousers, hair in scarves and straw hats, the men dressed any old how...

63

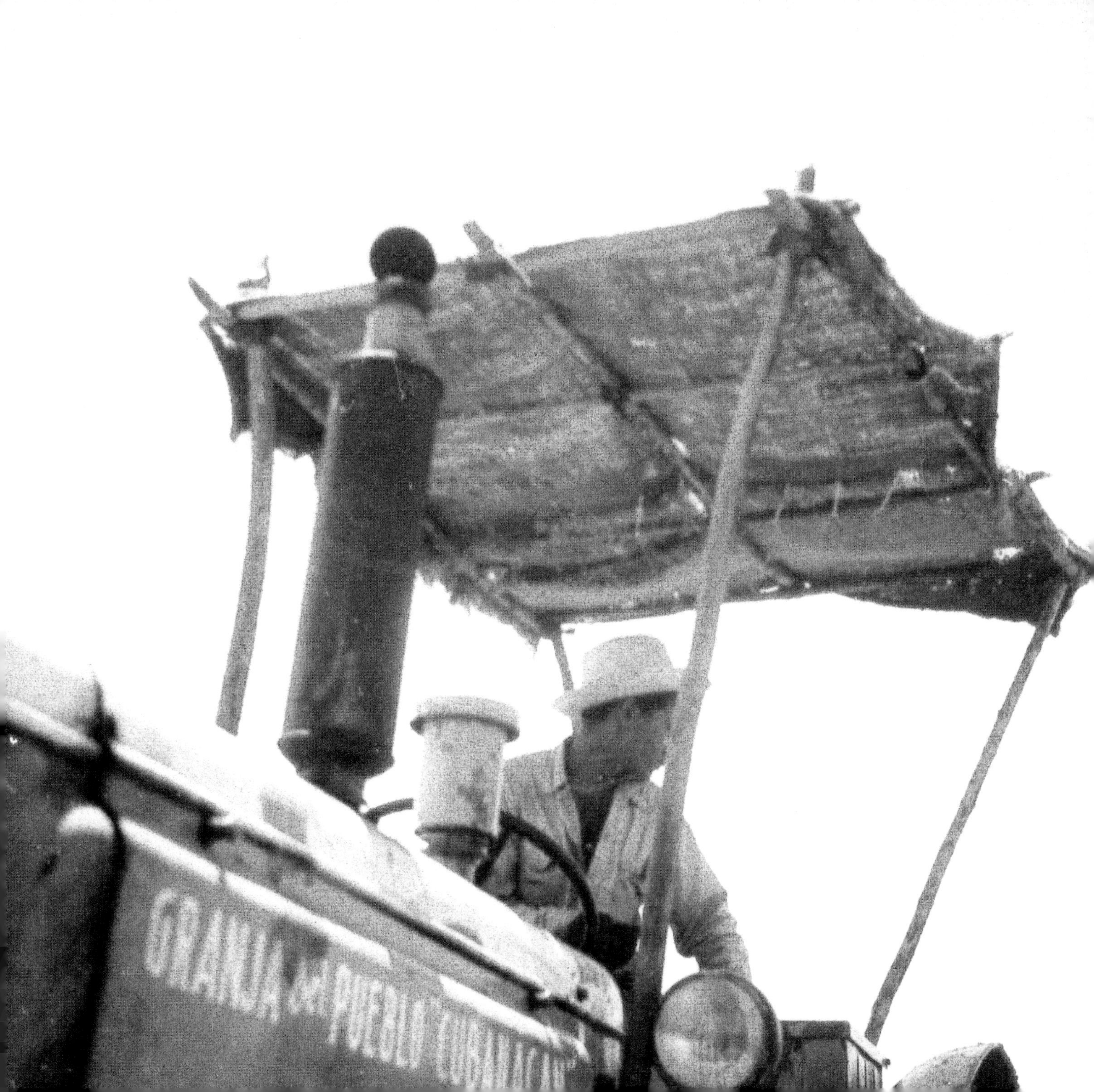
GRANJA del PUEBLO CUBANO

The lorries chug us through dawn in the suburbs, jungled with the scrapheaps of automobiles and the hoardings and signs – THIS FACTORY NOW BELONGS TO THE PEOPLE. After an hour, we drive through an arch of letters – THIS PEOPLE'S FARM GREETS THE 9TH ANNIVERSARY OF THE 26TH OF JULY (Castro's failed attack on the Moncada barracks in 1953). The student from INRA (in the planification department) insistently points out undistinguished landmarks. 'That is a school', indicating a building where I can see 'Escuela Antonio Guiteras' writ large on the front (all schools are now named after heroes of the Revolution). He plies me with sweets and drinks.

I look out to admire all the shades of green: olive green and viridian; dawn skies touched with green; chalky pastel greens like cake icing on the backs of the leaves; deep blue-greens in the shadows of the palms.

The landscape is like an extended oasis, expanded over the flat terrain bordered by hills; the view towards them broken only by the towering royal palms, lending an architectural perspective, elegantly spread among the green fields.

We aren't here to sow sugar cane, as expected, but to cut a field of maize.

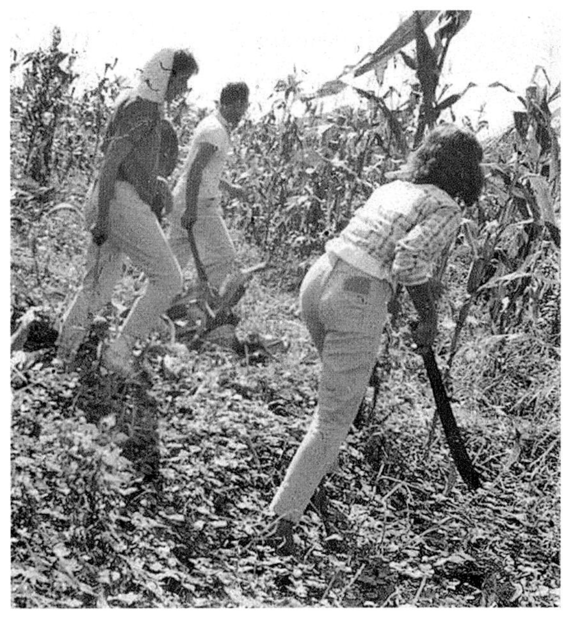

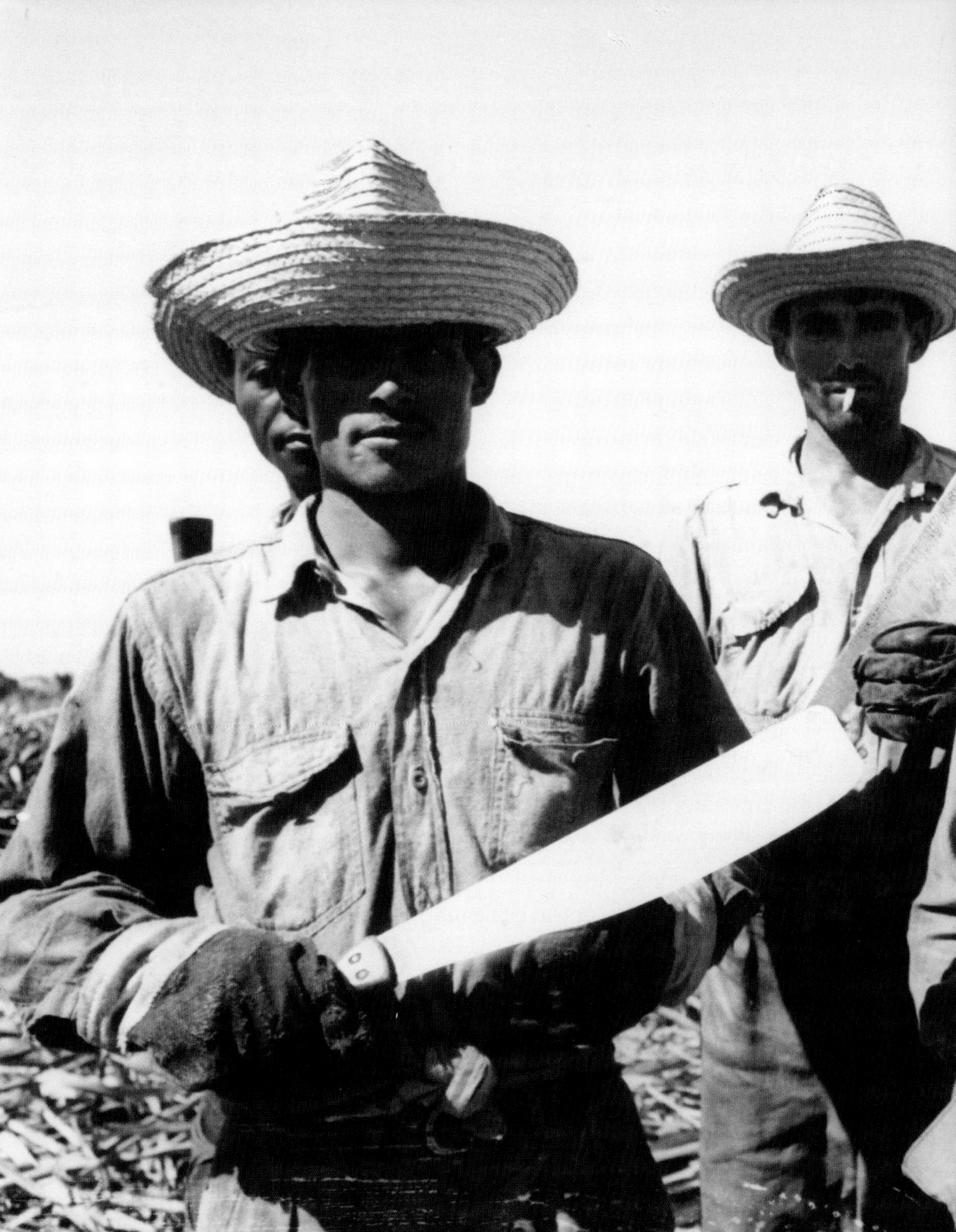

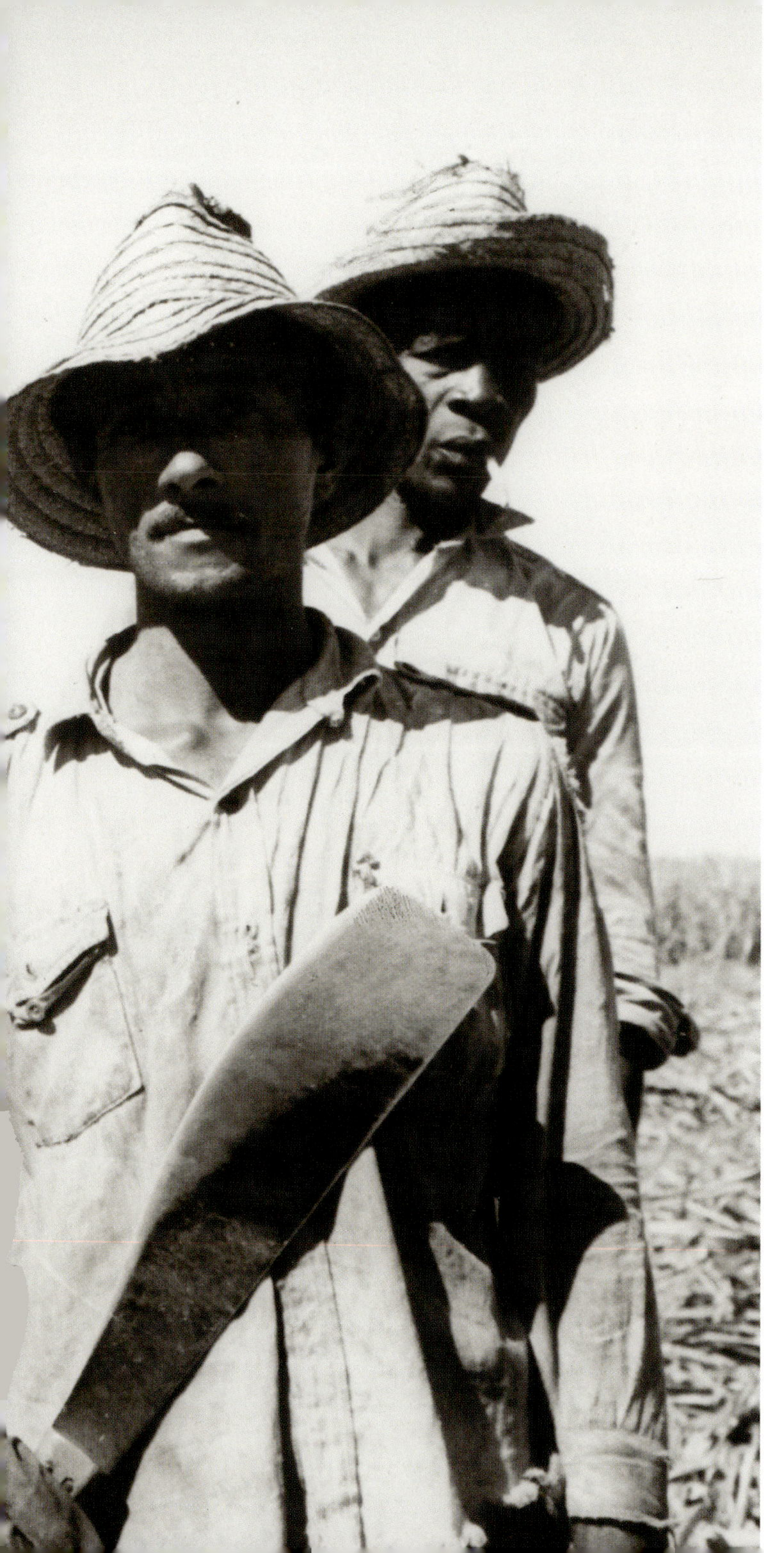

We engage in a fury of work. Antonio Salcines, one of the students, tosses a stalk in the air, dicing it with his machete as it falls: 'This is the enemy', he laughs. In one hour, ten acres have been razed. Gradually, the frenetic pace of work dissipates in sweat, thirst – due to the soft, blistered hands of the office workers. We gather in a shed by the road, seeking shade. An old man stands in the centre while we drink coffee and recites speeches and reads out bits of the newspaper; all this to lengthy applause. Russian lorries, with blond tartan-shirted drivers, pull over briefly to look.

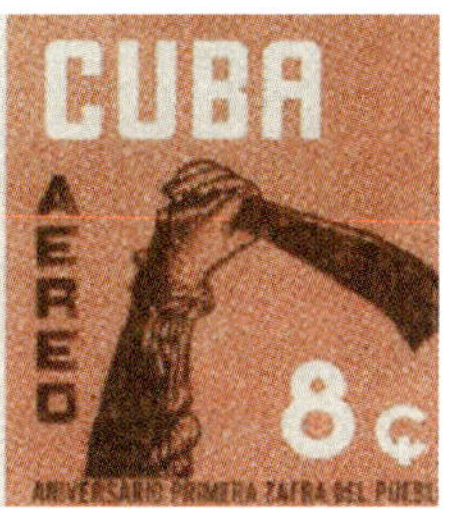

1962: Anniversary
of the first people's
sugar cane harvest

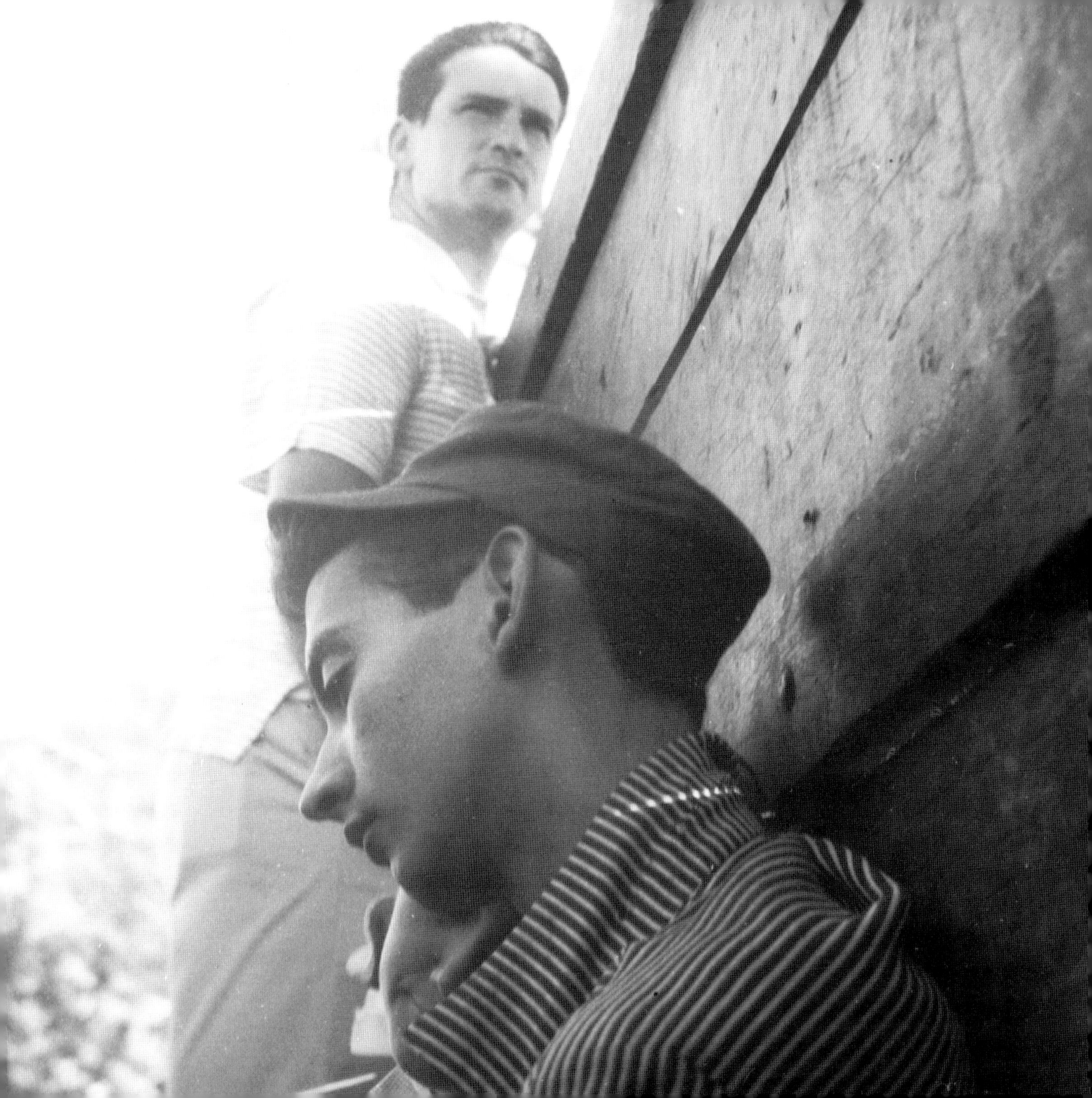

This man's dreaming. Or just sleeping. He probably didn't get to bed last night. Married only a fortnight ago. She's got her head on his shoulder, in the shadow – beautiful girl. He's very tired, but he's been 'emulating' in the spirit of the Revolution. That's what voluntary work's about – emulation. The INRA has a competition in emulation for workers in Comunicaciones, the government publishing arm.

Dear Tasha,
In the offices of Intercomunicaciones, a government propaganda agency, all they ever seem to do is chat and play pool. In a surreal turn of events, I have been asked to write something for <u>Pueblo y Cultura</u>, a local magazine, on the topic of 'ironwork balconies' (alas, they must not think me cut out for work in the fields).

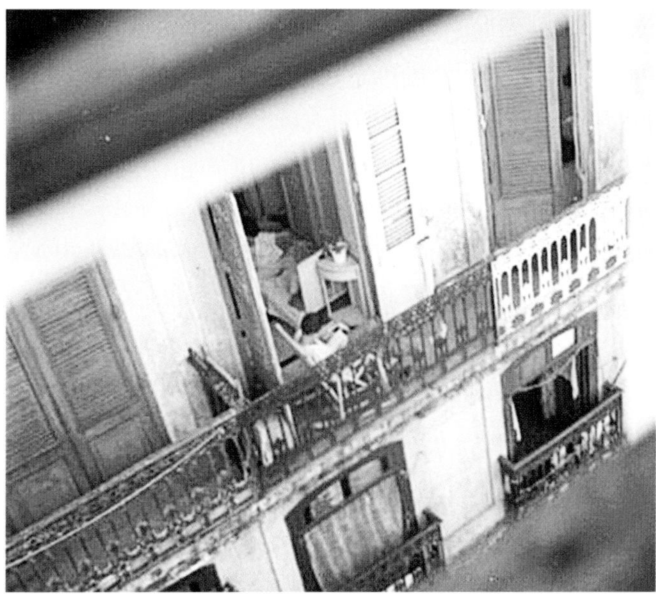

29 AUGUST. An American U-2 spy plane photographs eight launch sites under the command of Maj. Gen. Statsenko, western Cuba. Two days later, the director of the CIA informs Kennedy that this is definitive proof of the presence of Soviet-made surface-to-air missiles in Cuba (defensive missiles, rather than offensive ones).

Meanwhile, Che Guevara is with Khrushchev at his summer house in Yalta, Crimea, trying to persuade him to make a public declaration of his defence treaty with Cuba.

Kennedy favours a quick strike to take out the missile batteries; his brother, Robert, pushes for a staged attack on their own naval base at Guantánamo Bay, or the deliberate sinking of a US vessel, as pretext for a full invasion.

The cattle, bred for meat, grey, with lumps between their shoulders as if they dream of being camels; their skin somehow resembles the dry, cracked, hide of an elephant. Many stories about the growing meat shortages, fanciful explanations.

In the first years of the Revolution, the meat got better and better. But that's because they were slaughtering the young cattle, of which now there are few. Recently, thousands of dollars were paid for a bull from the US, but it was soon slaughtered for its meat. At a dairy farm, I am assured of the solidarity of the Canadians, so generous in supplying the milking machinery, even sending technicians to set it up. Rabid Yankee-hatred must have been expected to make me blind to the chrome plaque that clearly read 'Wisconsin'.

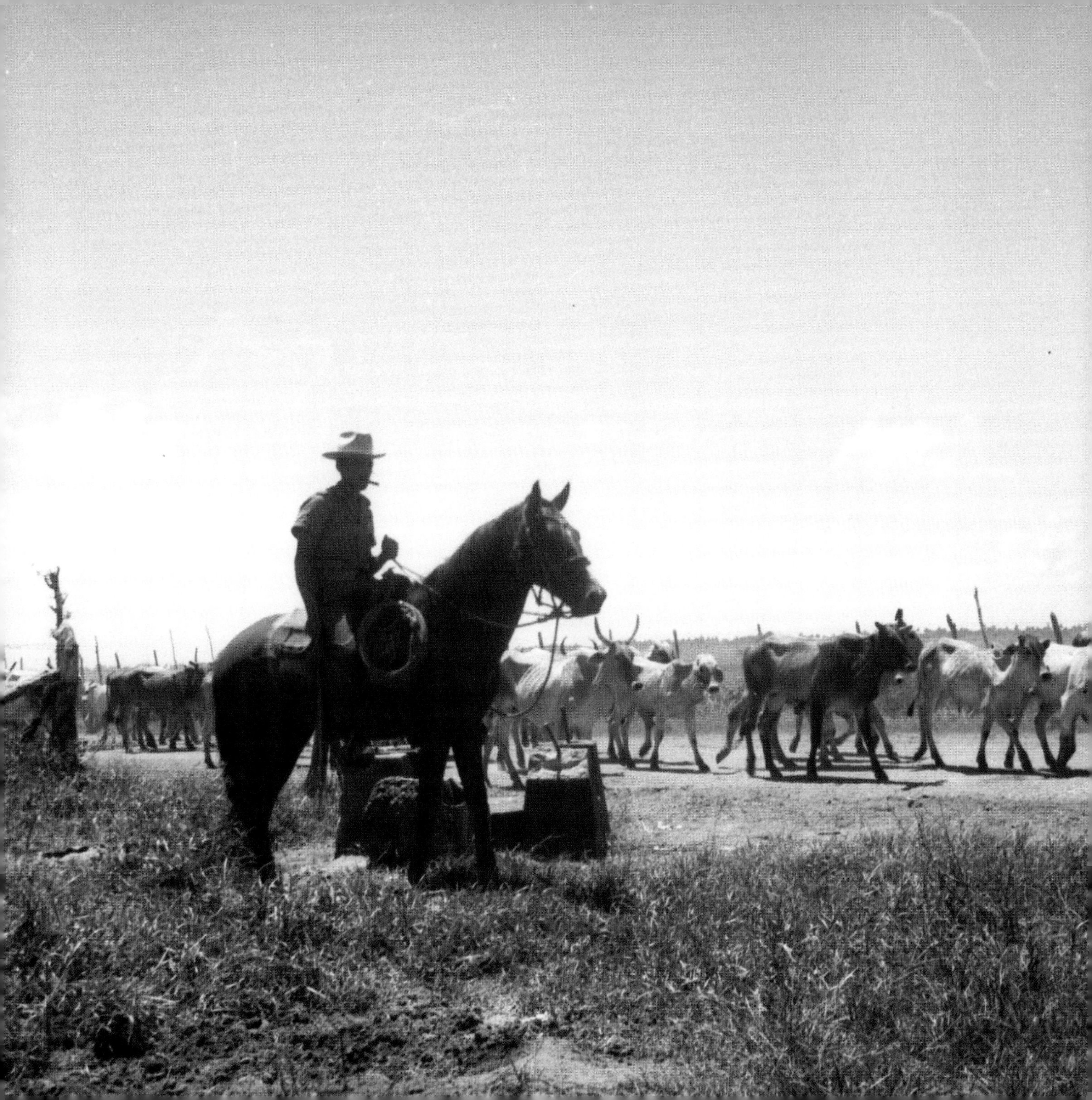

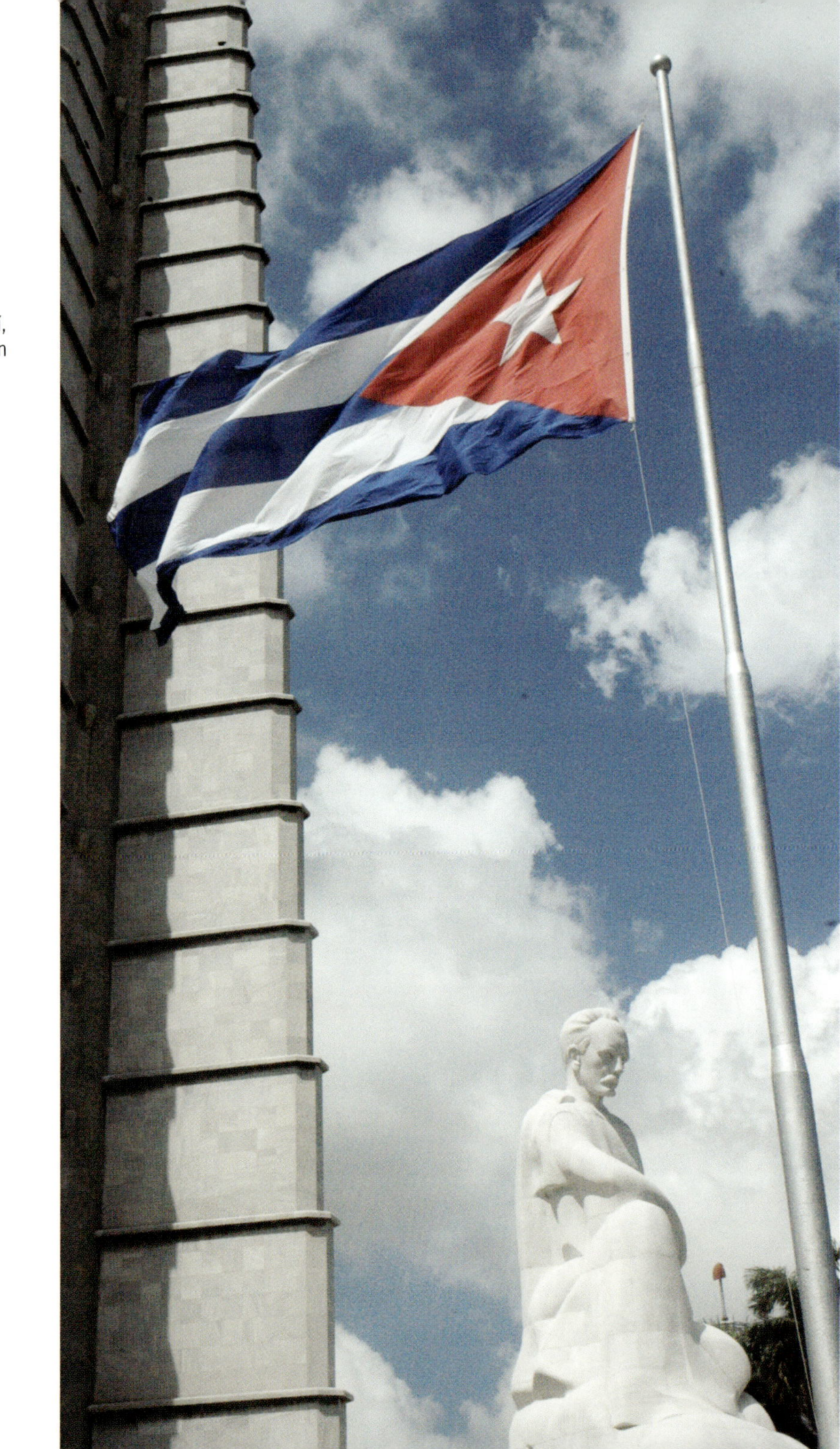

Monument to José Martí,
Plaza de la Revolución

Meetings at the Intercomunicaciones office. It stands on the Plaza Cívica, a few hundred yards away from the INRA headquarters, to which I've also been provided an introduction. The plaza — a huge open space surrounded by haphazard blocks of government buildings — is bisected by roads, making it almost impossible for a pedestrian to get from one building to another. At its heart, the wedding-cake column in honour of Jose Martí, 'the Apostle' of Cuban independence. Consul to Uruguay, Paraguay and Argentina in the late 1800s, he was killed riding a white charger against the Spanish occupiers, a book of poems in his pocket. Martí's collected works run to seventy volumes: poetry and journalism, a play and a novel. His name is invoked in every speech, and a quotation found in support of any measure. It's difficult to imagine that there would have been a revolution at all without Martí's example.

At Fidel's trial in 1953 he was able to quote huge chunks from Martí's writing. 'To be educated is to be free' was one of the mottos of the literacy campaign last year.

But let me tell you about seeing a speech by Fidel. Him, bear-like, coaxing and wheedling, crooning. Really quite fantastic: he is like a brilliant poet, no rabble rouser, building his argument slowly, questioningly; not someone cut out for the 20th century — but we shall see. More of which soon…

Sergio – the lead in *Memories of Underdevelopment* – has just come away from a debate on literature and politics. With a sharp jump-cut, the view transports us to him wandering alone across a huge expanse of concrete, agonising in voice-over. The camera rolls from the position of an aerial surveying shot, seemingly disembodied in a way that suggests Sergio is being surveilled by some authority beyond the human. (The shooting script specifies that he is cowed further by a billboard with a slogan by Trần Đức Thảo, an image which remained on the floor of the cutting-room.)

The camera tracks with him, slowly zooming until his image fills the frame, then loses focus: his physical outline becomes indistinct, dematerialising – like the rentier class he represents – in the newly rechristened Plaza de la Revolución.

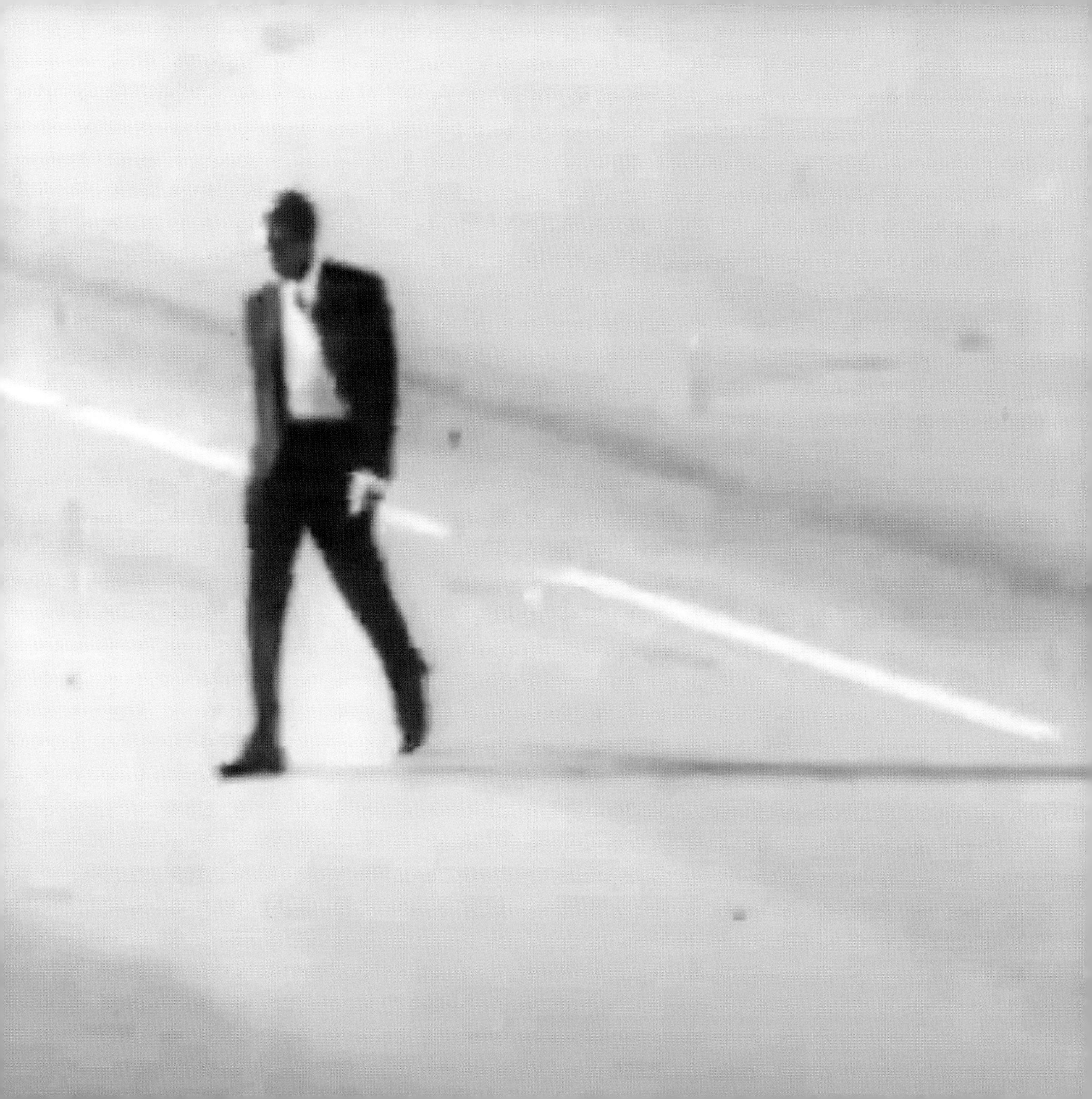

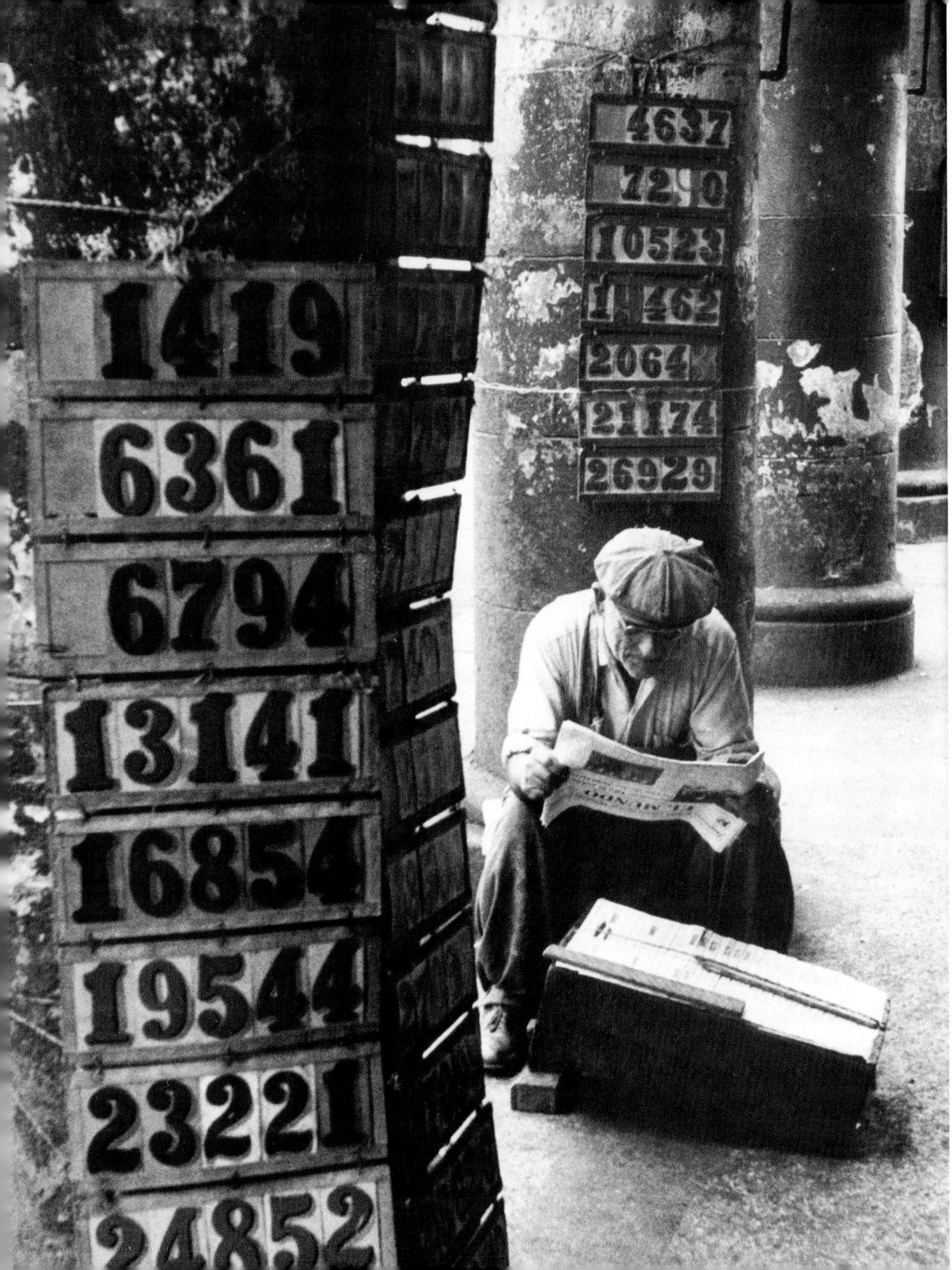

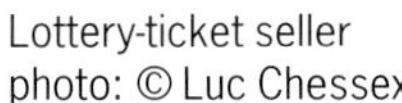

Lottery-ticket seller
photo: © Luc Chessex

Agnès Varda, who was in Cuba in 1962, captures in *Salut les Cubains* the arrival of a cargo boat under the flags of Cuba and Vietnam. Her film, a montage sequenced from among four thousand photographs taken during her stay, portrays the lottery vendors under the arcades on the Parque de la Fraternidad, the array of tickets fluttering in the wind. Before the Revolution, it is said, profits from the lottery lined the pockets of Batista's wife, but are now directed towards slum clearance and housing.

Varda documents the results of the literacy campaign, snaps a jaunty portrait of Raúl Castro and his comandantes Calixto García and Juan Almeida in the stern of the revolutionary yacht *Granma*. She photographs Fidel who 'is to Cuba what Gary Cooper is to the Western' and labels his guerrillas as *maquisards*. Varda bumps into Henri Cartier-Bresson in the corridor of her hotel, a place which never ran out of pineapples (for foreigners), even in such times of scarcity. *Salut les Cubains* is an image of a people in eternal, subtropical, bloom; its voice-over informs the viewer that the Cubans' march into revolution was 'to the step of the conga'.

Dear Tasha
Met my first bearded revolutionary yesterday in the Agricultural Reform Ministry. He was only twenty-three, I should think, and brusque to the point of mechanical. All the people there seem to be young, sitting at their executive desks. I suppose these were university students at the time of the Revolution (only those who were with Fidel in the Sierra Maestra wear beards – most of them have since shaved). I am taking as many photos as I can, but with caution. The British Consul told me it took him three weeks to get the last Englishman taking pictures out on bail.

There is trouble with my airline ticket. Iberia say it's not valid because not bought in Cuba. They won't refund the money and the National Bank won't let money in without stealing about half, they're so desperate for dollars. Had good time out for dinner with Tony last night. We met Siné, the French cartoonist, very small and young and looking very wealthy in Cuban company. We listened to yet another history of the glorious revolution. The story of what they call Playa Girón, the attempted invasion. Listened to more marvellous Cuban music … Going out again this evening with an <u>El Mundo</u> journalist and family … Thursday to a cooperative farm … If the Cubans can survive the economic blockade, I can't see that they have anything to worry about. Of course, I haven't yet seen the other side of the Revolution. The young man at the INRA told me that capitalists would not open their shops at the weekend and thought this was monstrous, whether or not a shop is nationalised.

5 SEPTEMBER. Khrushchev is informed that the US is now fully aware of the Soviet military presence in Cuba. He is shocked, having hoped that the bases would not be noticed until after the US mid-term congressional elections in November, when he was planning to unveil his move – in dramatic fashion – at the UN General Assembly. None of the ballistic missiles have yet been unloaded, nor primed with warheads. There is still time to pull back, de-escalate. Instead, within two days, the Soviet premier orders that six bombers, carrying atomic charges, immediately be sent to Cuba alongside divisions of missiles with twelve warheads.

Officially, General Pliev is not permitted to use nuclear weapons without express authorisation from Khrushchev; but instructions are drawn up in Moscow to allow him to use tactical (short-range) nuclear missiles in the event of a land invasion of Cuba. As during the Bay of Pigs invasion, Che Guevara is put in command of Cuba's western army in Pinar del Río, the area of the island closest to the United States.

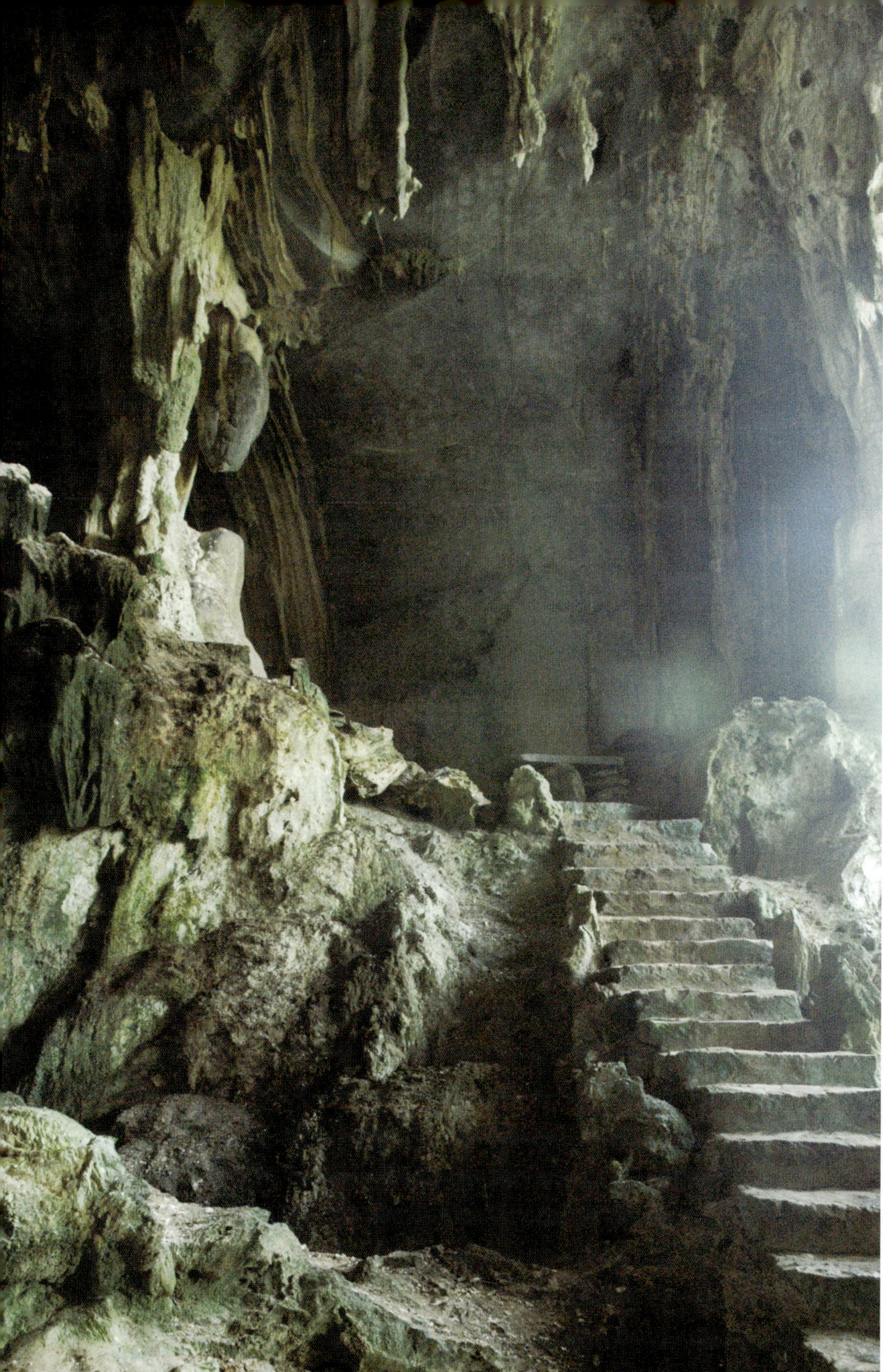

Che Guevara's command post during
Missile Crisis, Sierra de los Órganos

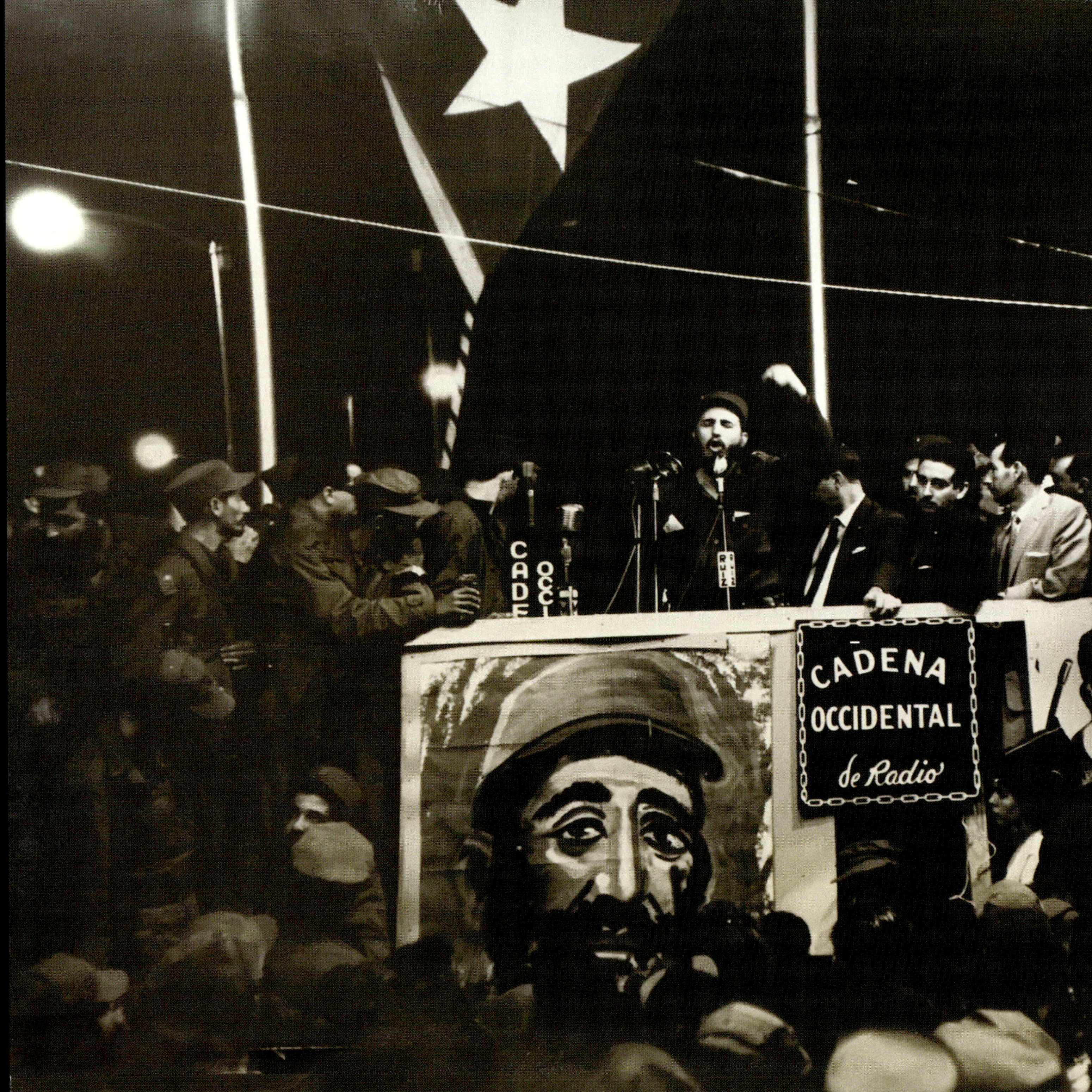

CADENA
OCCIDENTAL
de Radio

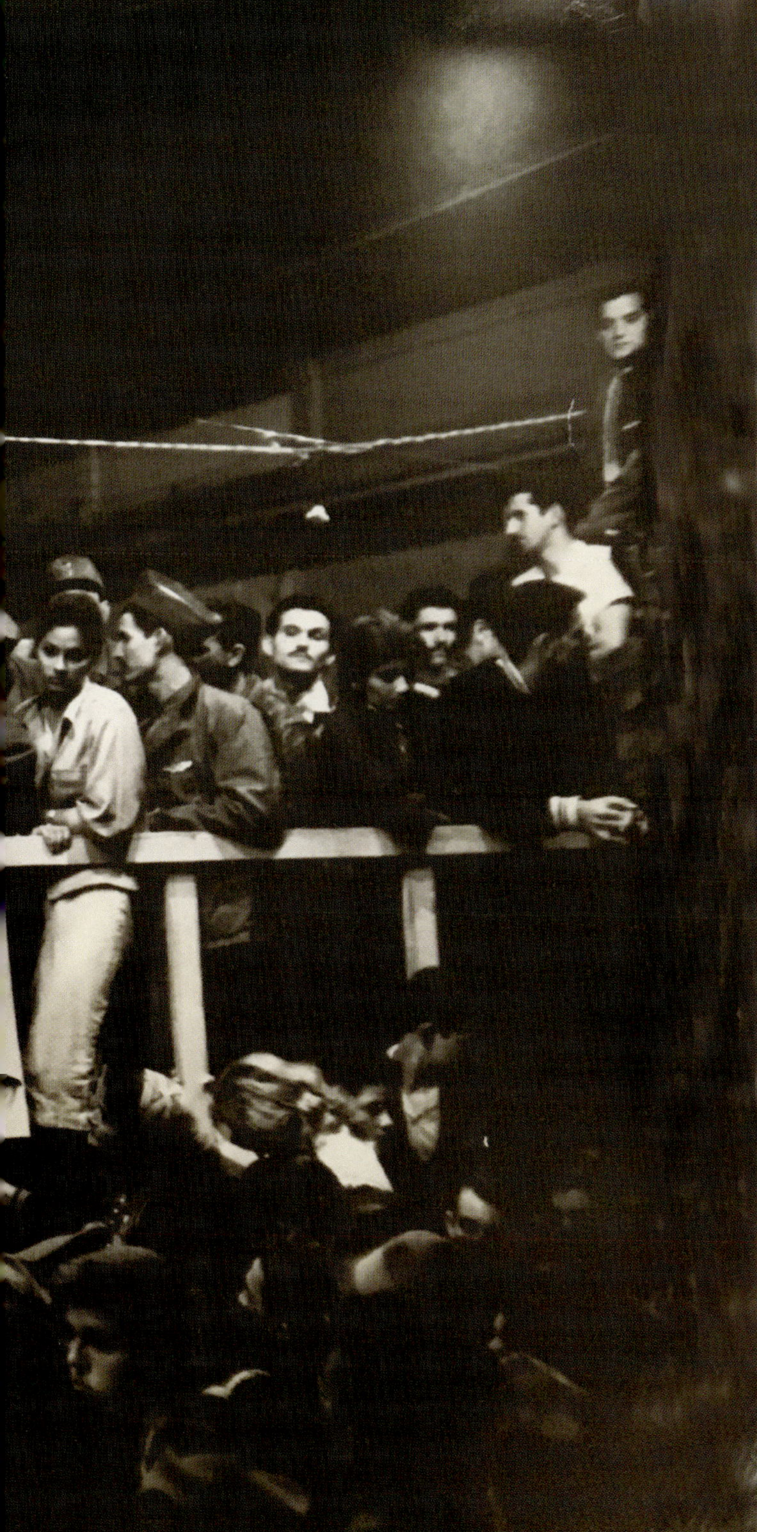

Castro speaking, first week of Revolution, eastern Cuba.
Photo © Andrew St. George

11 SEPTEMBER. Last night, the annual Congress of Education: Fidel. Us: sitting in the cavernous Chaplin Theatre (rechristened the Carlos Marx) in the outskirts, sitting out dull speeches and eulogies. Much like a Sunday night at the Palladium, tolerating tiresome warm-up acts for Frankie Vaughan. The tacit understanding: there is only one star. Reminds me of the British magazine with a photo of the singer in the bath, labelled 'Isn't he a cuddly little teddy bear?' Well, Fidel presents himself as a lovable bear with oiled joints and voice. Heads of various councils and committees report on progress, etc. All the while, delegates from the Union of Young Communists murmur, shout and agitate. Fidel sits loose-limbed and laid back on the podium, turns around to conduct a conversation, scans through a stack of papers.

Shouts of FI-DEL, FI-DEL, FI-DEL
mount like a wave in the hall;
furious flag-waving and fist pumps.
By eleven, the tension is eased by
the interruption of formal,
martial, music. Fidel under lights
at the rostrum. Absolute silence
seeps across the room. Out of which
his voice flows, undulating,
insistent, cajoling, looping back,
forward, repetitive. Brief summary
of work in literacy. Lengthy
exposition of threats posed by the
US, sovereignty, the Bay of Pigs.
Rousing, persuasive.

   'This work of the Revolution has
gone on under the most trying
circumstances, in the midst of a
revolutionary process, in the face
of aggression, hostility from
reactionary elements, the
machinations of imperialism. How
can they expect Cuba not to defend
itself, take all necessary measures
to protect ourselves, right down to
the last drop of blood?'
Spontaneous shouts from the
audience of 'Cuba Si, Yanqui No'.

11 SEPTEMBER. The TASS news agency disseminates a message from the Soviet command affirming they will defend Cuba in the wake of any attack on her sovereignty.

It is so hot the Russian soldiers sleep under wettened sheets. Over the next weeks, in a mounting atmosphere of fear fed by inaction, dissent spreads among the troops. The camps are poorly camouflaged and a pre-emptive strike could come at any moment. Any of the overflights could herald an invasion. Serious suggestions are made to stand the missiles on end, to make them look like palm trees. The incomparable taste of mango develops into an obsession.

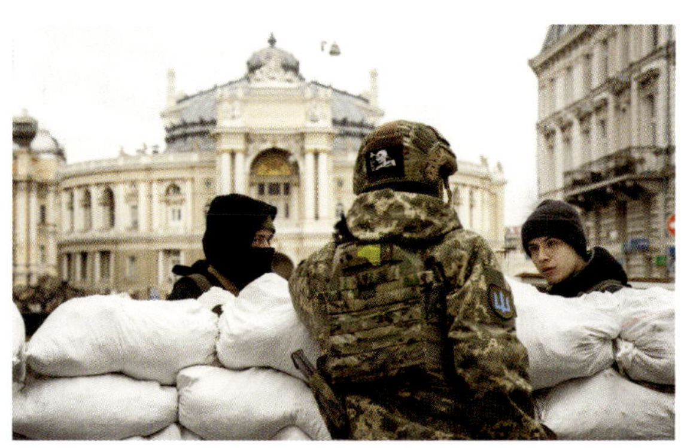

Ukrainian soldiers at barricade protecting Odesa's opera house, March 2022. The opera house came under attack by Bolsheviks in *Battleship Potemkin*
photo: © Alfons Cabrera

Tinned rations, not meant for such a climate, begin to go off; swarms of maggots writhe among the sacks of pasta and oats. For the men, it recalls the scene in Eisenstein's *Battleship Potemkin*, the flyblown side of beef their superiors force the crew to eat and make soup from until, the sailors having refused, the captain orders several executions. A mutiny is sparked; the officers and priest are hurled overboard. The ringleader dies, his body delivered solemnly on a tug into the port of Odesa as to a Bolshevik Valhalla. A sign is placed around his neck: not King of the Jews, but Killed for a Bowl of Soup. His body, laid out on the pier, becomes an object of veneration and soon, fired by injustice, the whole city is risen. After the Cossacks murder scores of women and children, the *Potemkin* turns its guns on Odesa's grand opera house, symbol of imperial decadence.

CIA estimates put the number of Soviet personnel in Cuba at around four thousand, and continue to push Kennedy to invade the island on the basis of this figure. (It is not until the 1990s that the US discovers the Soviets had deployed 43,000 men to Cuba.) The Soviet arms are still considered to be of a defensive nature, and certainly not nuclear. In real fact, following an invasion, Russian commanders in Cuba are ready to make a pre-emptive strike, which will automatically trigger mutual nuclear destruction. An American businessman is given an audience with Khrushchev during which he is told a parable about a goat. There was once a man who didn't like how his goat smelled, but eventually had to learn to live with it. The Soviet Union has endured the whiff of goats from Turkey and Italy, now the US has a goat in Cuba.

15 SEPTEMBER. Departure.
At the harbour, scores of refugees
with a single change of clothes,
clutching their $5 allowance.
Sat under murals of youth,
forward-marching,
beneath the Cuban flag
whose stripes blend or
dissolve into the sea.

Flies are fidgeting in the tears of
those saying goodbye. Outside the
waiting room, a troupe of girl
recruits for the militia is
drilling up and down, out of step.

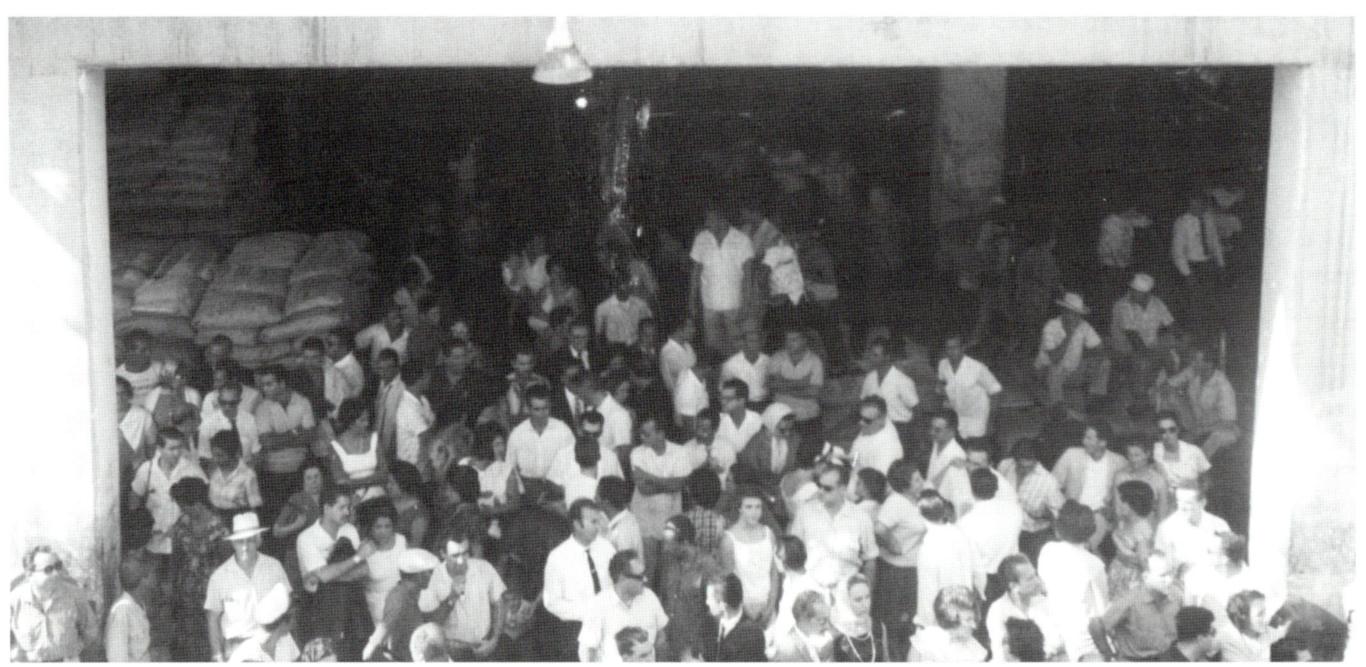

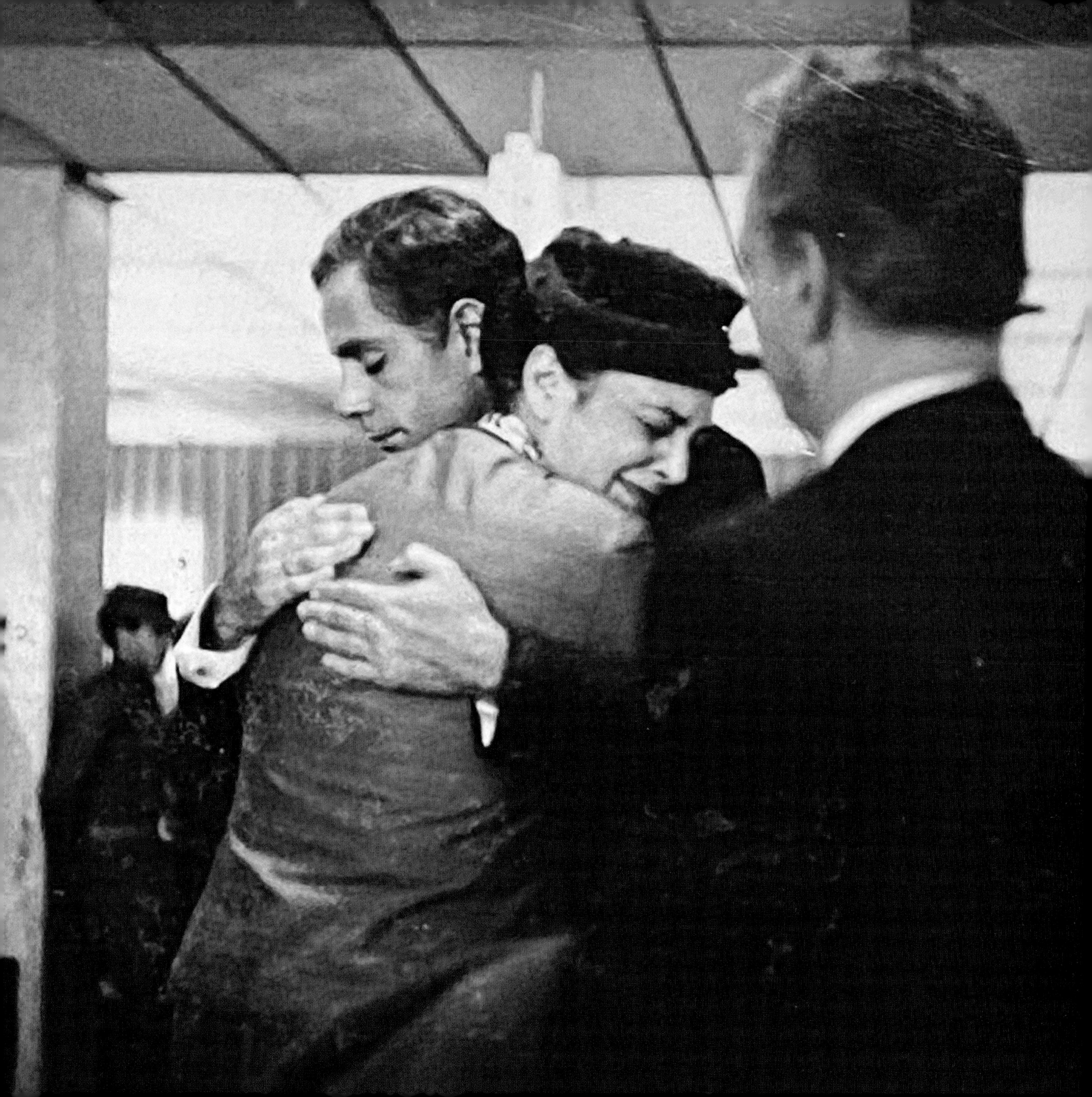

4 OCTOBER. The first nuclear warheads enter Cuba, at the port of Mariel, aboard the *Indigirka*. Further shipments of liquid fuel and missile components arrive at Bahía Honda and Casilda. Sixty nuclear charges, in total, for both the R-12 and the R-14 missiles. Each warhead has an explosive power similar to that of the bomb dropped on Hiroshima in 1945.

Before firing, the missiles need to be fuelled for two and a half hours, out in the open on the launch pads, making them highly vulnerable to attack. For safety, the warheads are stored in an underground bunker south of Havana, at least four hours' drive from most of the camps. At no point is American intelligence ever aware of the twelve tactical (range: 20 miles) Luna nuclear missiles positioned in the hills surrounding the US naval base at Guantánamo Bay, which remain on the island throughout – even beyond – the crisis.

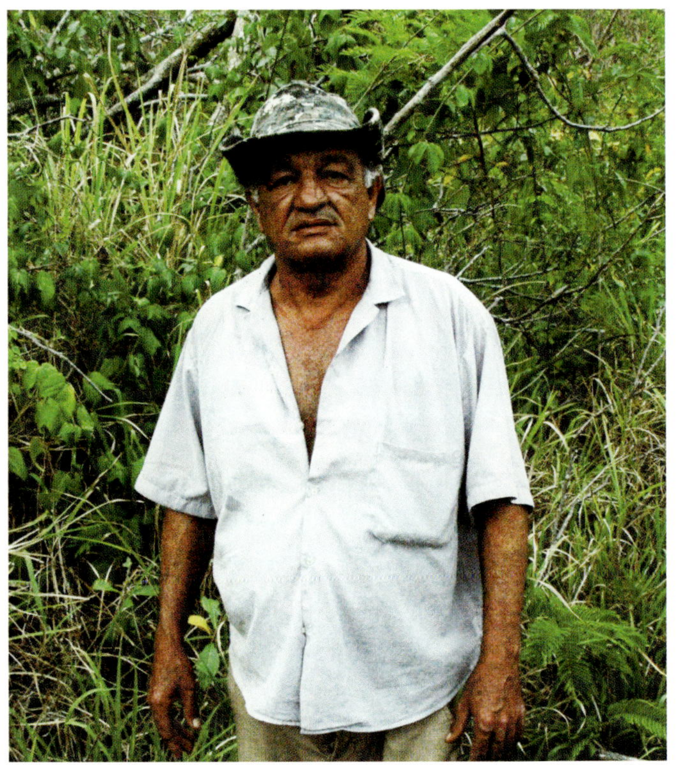

Manuel Iscariote
farmer of land at former missile site,
El Purio, central Cuba

8 OCTOBER. Colonel Sidorov's men at El Purio, perhaps still inspired by watching repeats of *And Quiet Flows the Don*, are the first to complete the assembly of their missile launch sites. Sidorov's whole regiment is combat-ready one week later, well ahead of schedule. Patriotic speeches are delivered atop a makeshift podium made from sacks full of Russian earth, with a striped border marker in the ground. Soon after Statsenko's (the lover of poetry) entire regiment in western Cuba declares itself, too, fully primed for action. Two days later, aboard the *Gagarin*, further munitions sail from the port of Mykolaiv in Ukraine.

Under the command of Colonel Ivan Sidorov, El Purio was the first of the six camps for R-12s to receive its missiles and the first on the island to declare itself battle-ready. (Some sources say this was the only base to which nuclear warheads were delivered, on the night of 26 October, 1962, making it the world's most dangerous flashpoint at that moment.)

14 OCTOBER. US reconnaissance planes photograph the camps at El Cacho and Santa Cruz de los Pinos, western Cuba, which they dub San Cristóbal 1 and 2. The next day, these are positively identified as launch sites for medium-range nuclear R-12s, capable of striking Washington, DC.

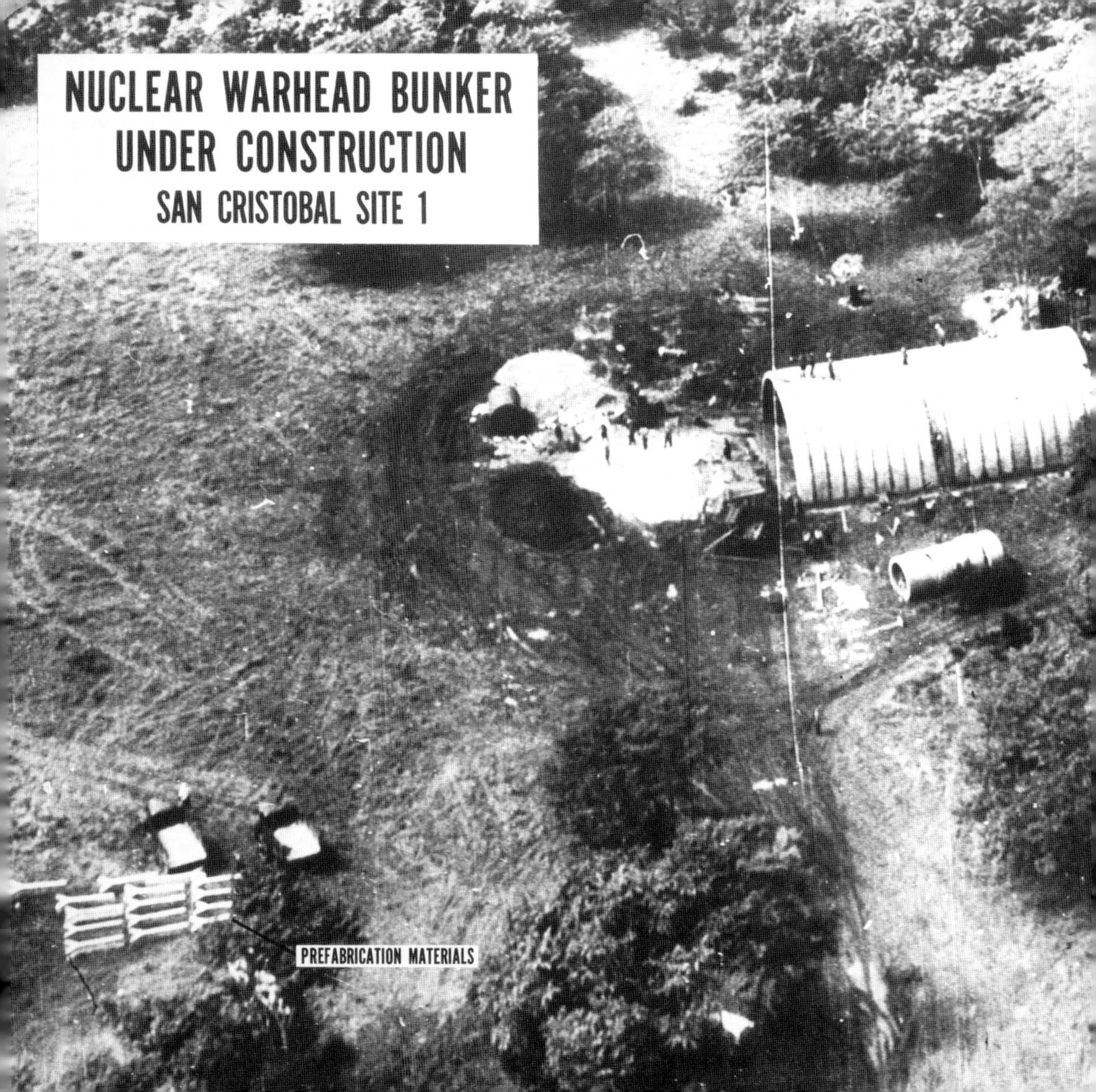
NUCLEAR WARHEAD BUNKER
UNDER CONSTRUCTION
SAN CRISTOBAL SITE 1
PREFABRICATION MATERIALS

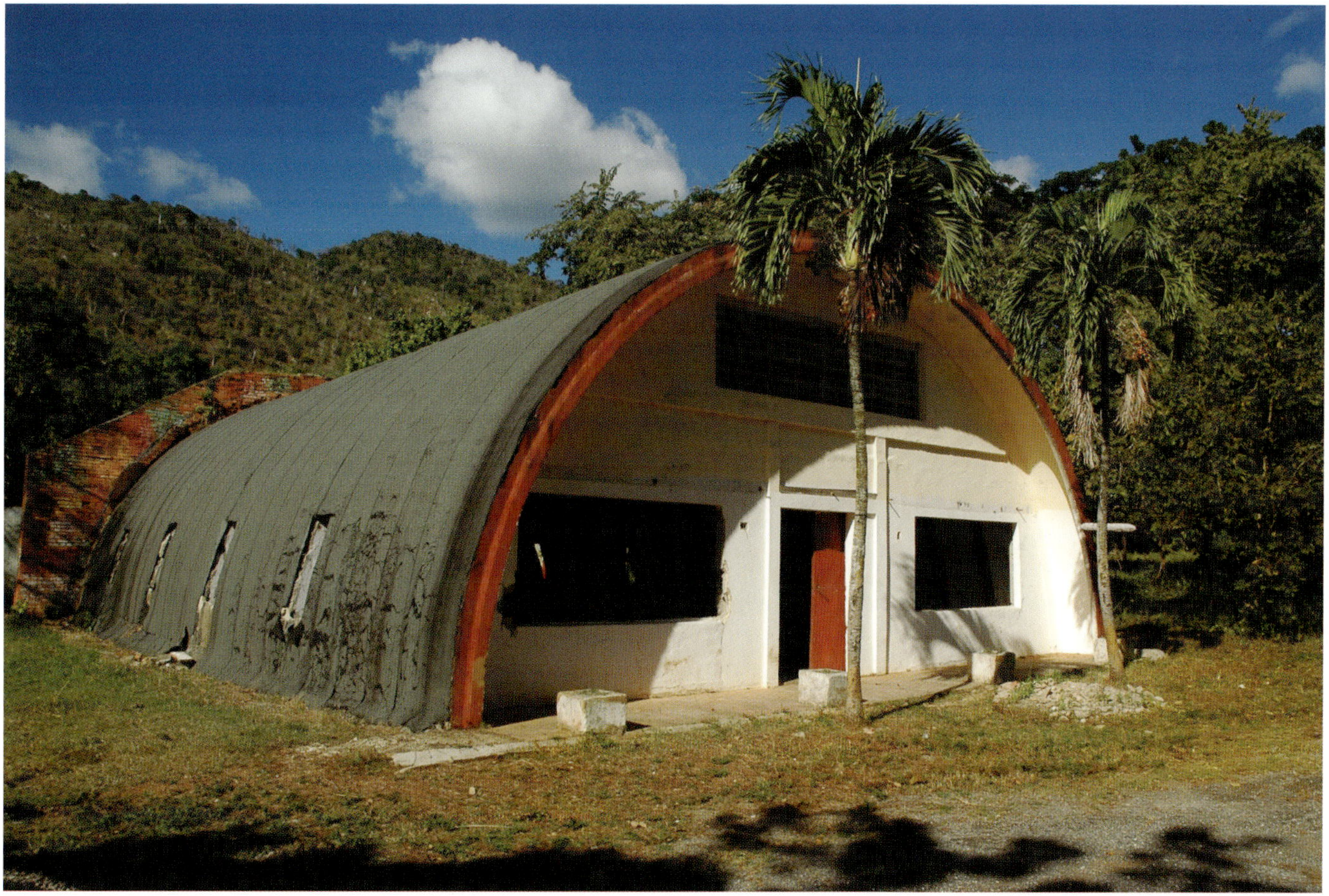

Hangar at El Cacho (San Cristóbal 1), one of only two structures remaining from 1962

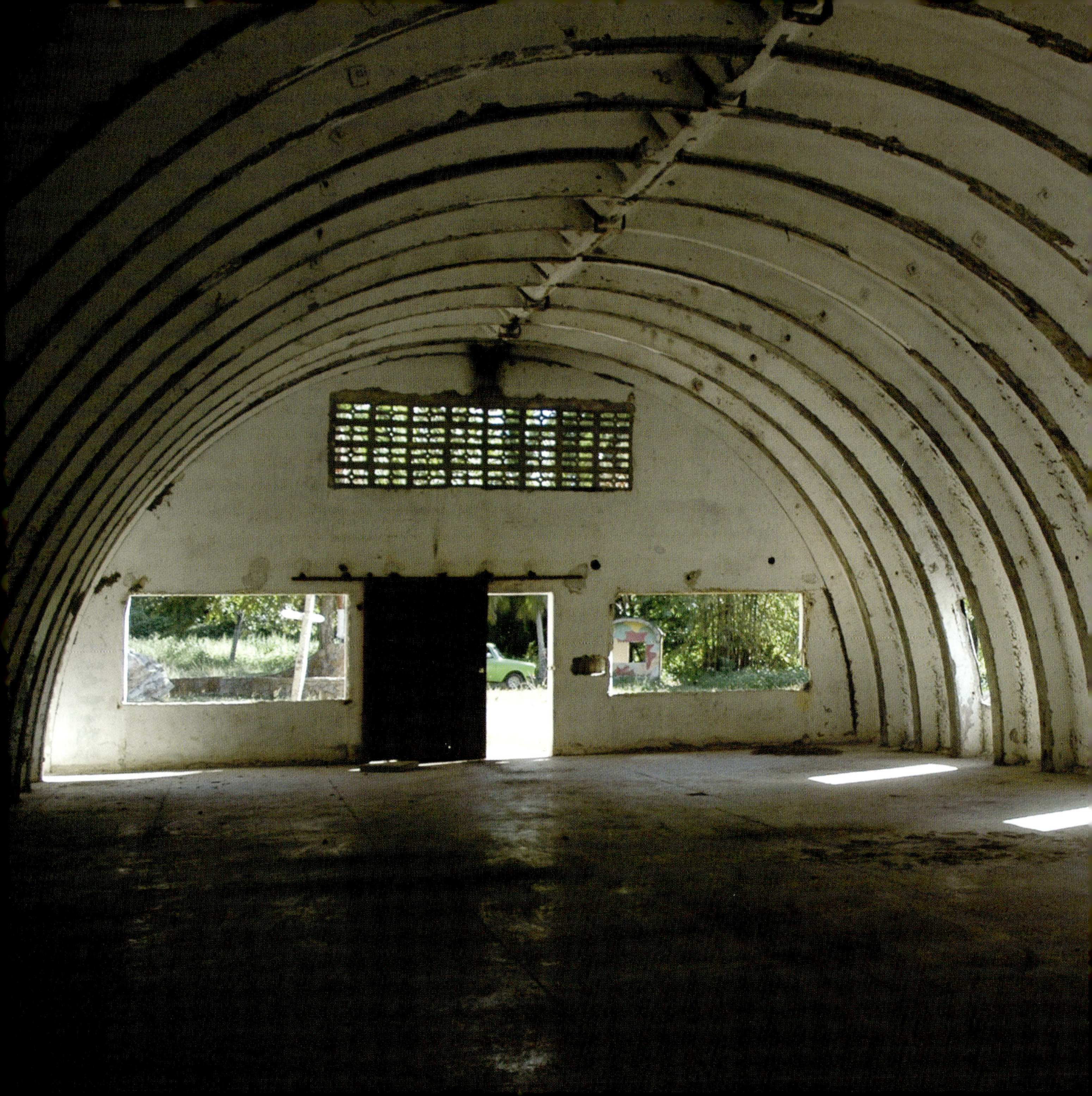

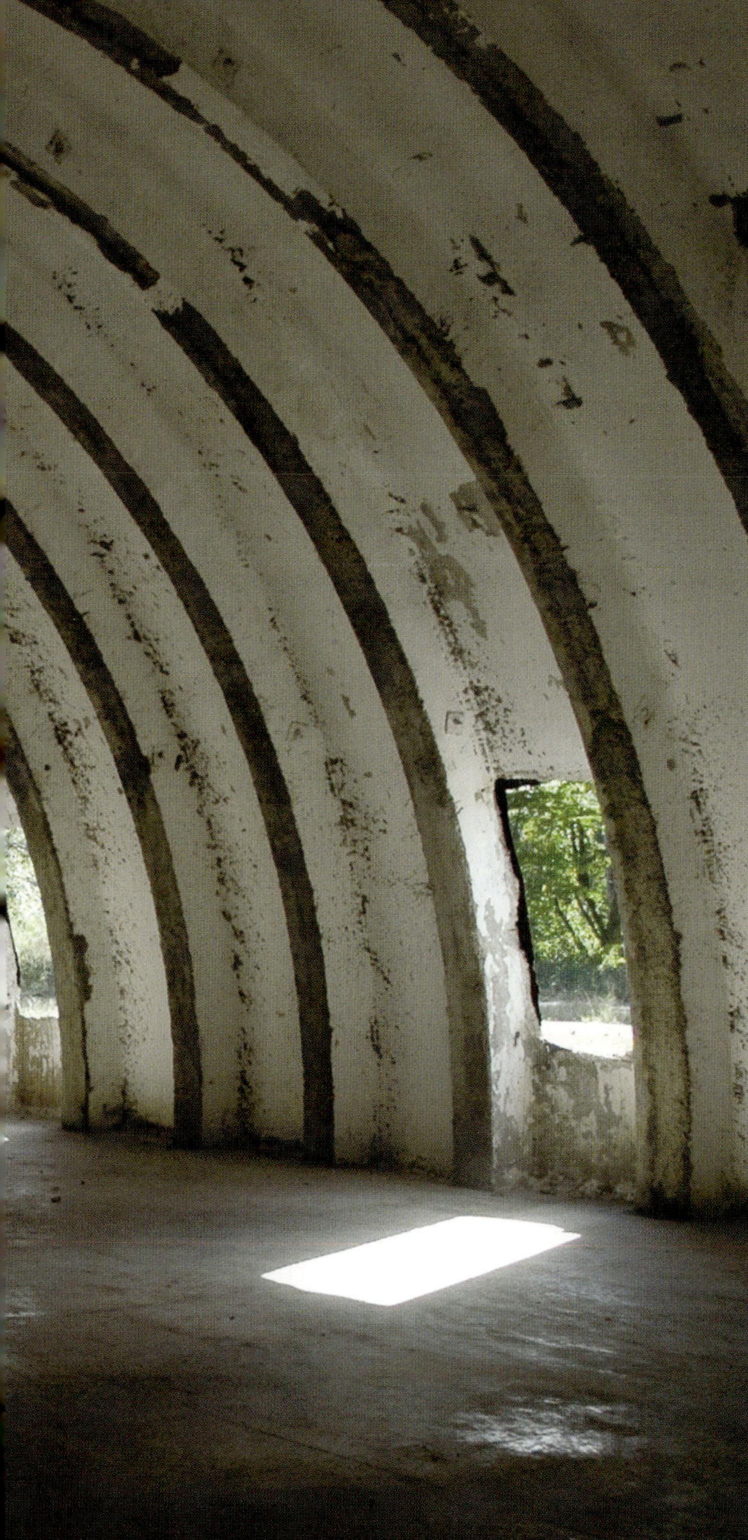

This 25-metre-long hangar, made from 44 reinforced concrete arches, stood originally at the headquarters of the USSR's 43rd Missile Division at Kremenchuk, present-day Ukraine. It arrived at the Cuban port of Mariel on 16 September 1962 and was reassembled, by night, at El Cacho, made to house six missiles. These hangars were climate-controlled and, inside, R-12s would have been armed by connecting the missile body to the warhead before being transported to the launchpad. In hot, eastern, Cuba – where they were still uncommon – air-conditioning units had to be requisitioned from local brothels to cool the liquid fuel and warheads. This building was the first to be discovered by US spy planes, and was briefly the centre of the world's attention when a photograph of it was displayed at an emergency meeting of the UN Security Council on October 25, 1962.

At the end of the crisis, in accordance with directives from the UN, all trace of the Soviet camps was to be erased. But, mysteriously (perhaps due to the speed of their withdrawal) two missile hangars were left intact, the only structures remaining from the period.

16 OCTOBER. Early in the morning, scanning the newspapers in bed with some freshly squeezed orange juice, Kennedy is informed by his security advisor that photographs confirm the presence of offensive Soviet missiles in Cuba. The American president is reminded that a nuclear war would entail the deaths of seventy million US citizens, nearly half the population. Almost the entirety of Kennedy's Executive Committee, CIA, Chiefs of Staff, and advisors (the most belligerent among them being his brother, Robert) again push for a massive strike on Cuba, followed by a land invasion. Kennedy holds steady.

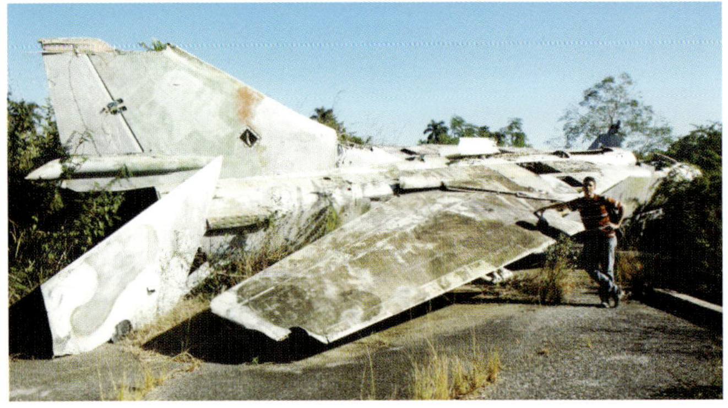

Wreck of Soviet MiG-21, El Cacho.
Once able to fly up to 60,000 feet at speeds of 1,000 mph, armed with infra-red missiles and cannon.
One of the forty-two MiG-21s delivered in August, 1962.

22 OCTOBER. Kennedy delivers a televised speech, informing the world and announcing a naval blockade of Cuba. From two days' time, any ship entering a zone five hundred nautical miles off the island will be intercepted and searched. Strategic Air Command units are given the order to raise their Defense Readiness Condition (DEFCON) to Level 2, the first time this has ever happened; Level 1 is for conditions of open warfare. A squadron of 1,500 bombers is readied to attack with an arsenal of 2,962 nuclear warheads. Seventy-two nuclear-armed B-52s immediately take to the air, circulating. Cuba's Revolutionary Armed Forces are made combat-ready. People's Defence units mobilised as combat battalions and firefighters. Cuban civilians start signing up for first-aid training in hospitals. Volunteer militias are instructed to round up suspected counter-revolutionaries who are then interned in makeshift prisons, basketball courts. Unidentified US ships appear, dark smudges on the horizon. Anti-aircraft batteries are installed at elevated points across Havana, on the seafront; they bristle among the palmettos in the terraced gardens of opulent Hotel Nacional, above the swimming pool on the roof terrace of the Hotel Capri. Coastal defence cruise missile installations are mounted around the island.

23 OCTOBER. Publicly, Khrushchev gives the order that any ship not over the blockade line before the deadline of 10.00 EST/14.00 GMT the following day is to turn back for the USSR. Privately, he urges the *Aleksandrovsk* (containing sixty-eight warheads) to press on towards Cuba. Following Kennedy's speech, it is assumed an invasion is imminent and all Soviet divisions across Cuba are put on high alert. Not for the last time, Castro urges Khrushchev to launch a pre-emptive nuclear strike against any expeditionary force, a request that deeply unsettles the Soviet leader. Castro appears on Cuban radio and television to suggest the Soviets will not tolerate the US position, rejecting many of the statements made by Kennedy.

★

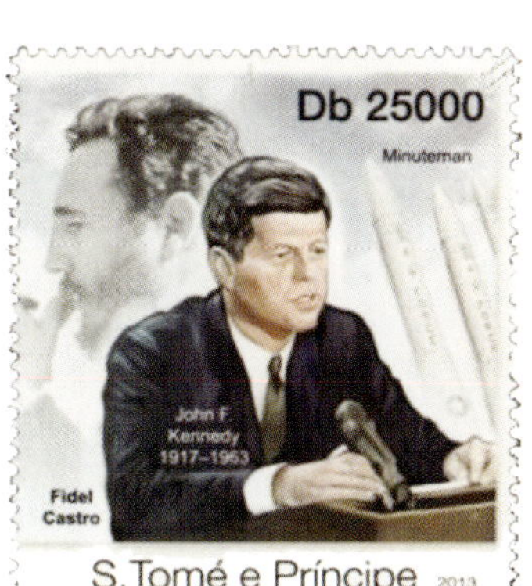

25 OCTOBER. In New York, at a special meeting of the Security Council, the Soviet representative to the UN dismisses claims of the presence of offensive missiles in Cuba as 'fake evidence'. Adlai Stevenson, the US representative, in a scene reminiscent of Graham Greene's *Our Man in Havana* – published four years prior – unveils photographs of the missile bases at El Cacho ('San Cristóbal 1') and Santa Cruz de Los Pinos ('San Cristóbal 2'), the missile hangar.

Tense, secret negotiations begin in which Khrushchev suggests to Kennedy that he is willing to remove his ballistic missiles from Cuba in exchange for the latter's promise not to invade the island. The Cuban government is not consulted. The Soviet premier seeks such assurances, not so much out of concern for Cuban sovereignty, but to show the world he has exacted a price from Kennedy in the negotiations; more crucially, he now feels the likelihood of events spinning out of his control. The number of Soviet troops in Cuba, even alongside the Cuban military, could never withstand a full-blown assault by the United States. It will then prove impossible to prevent the use of his tactical nuclear missiles against an invading ground force.

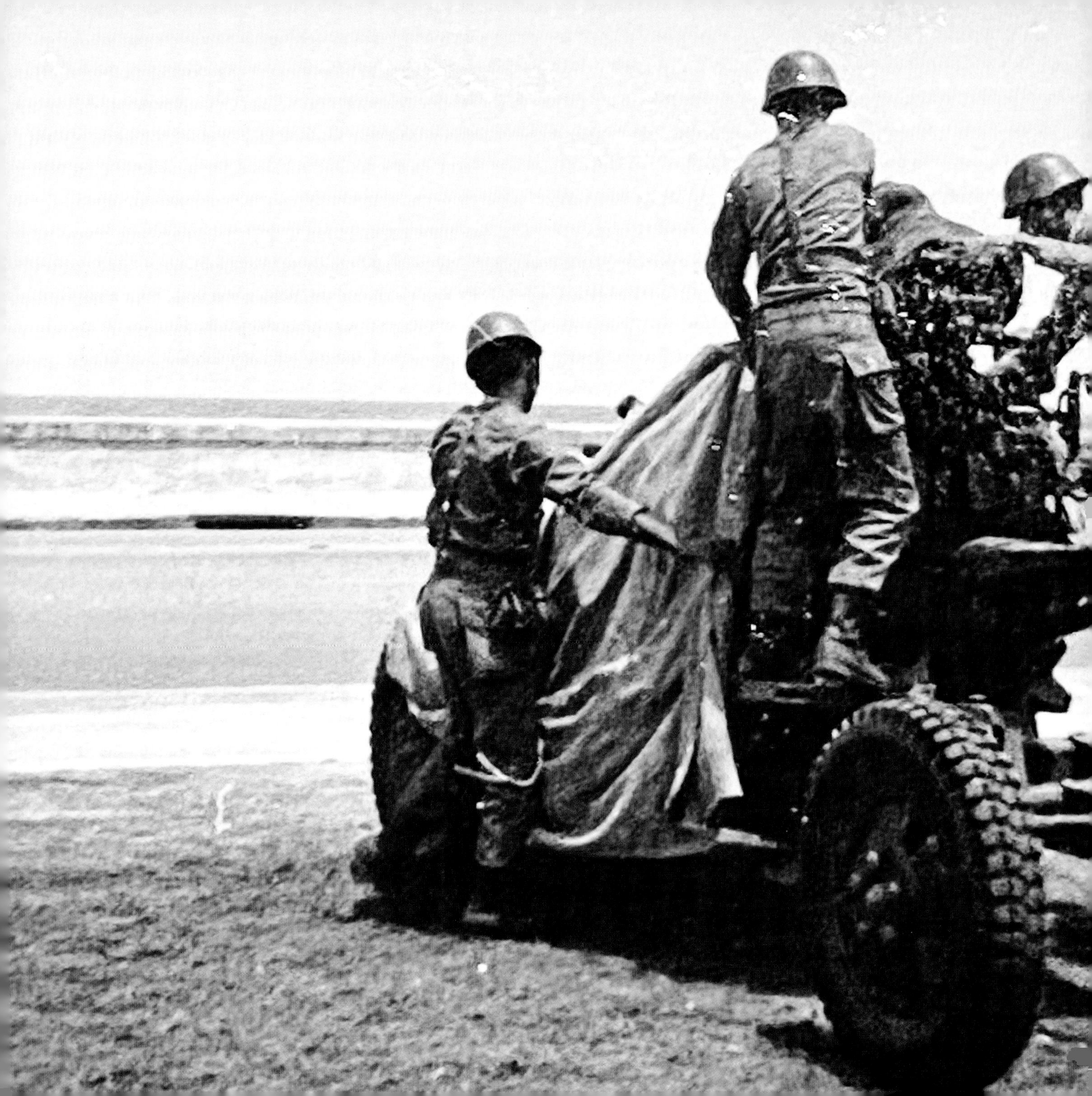

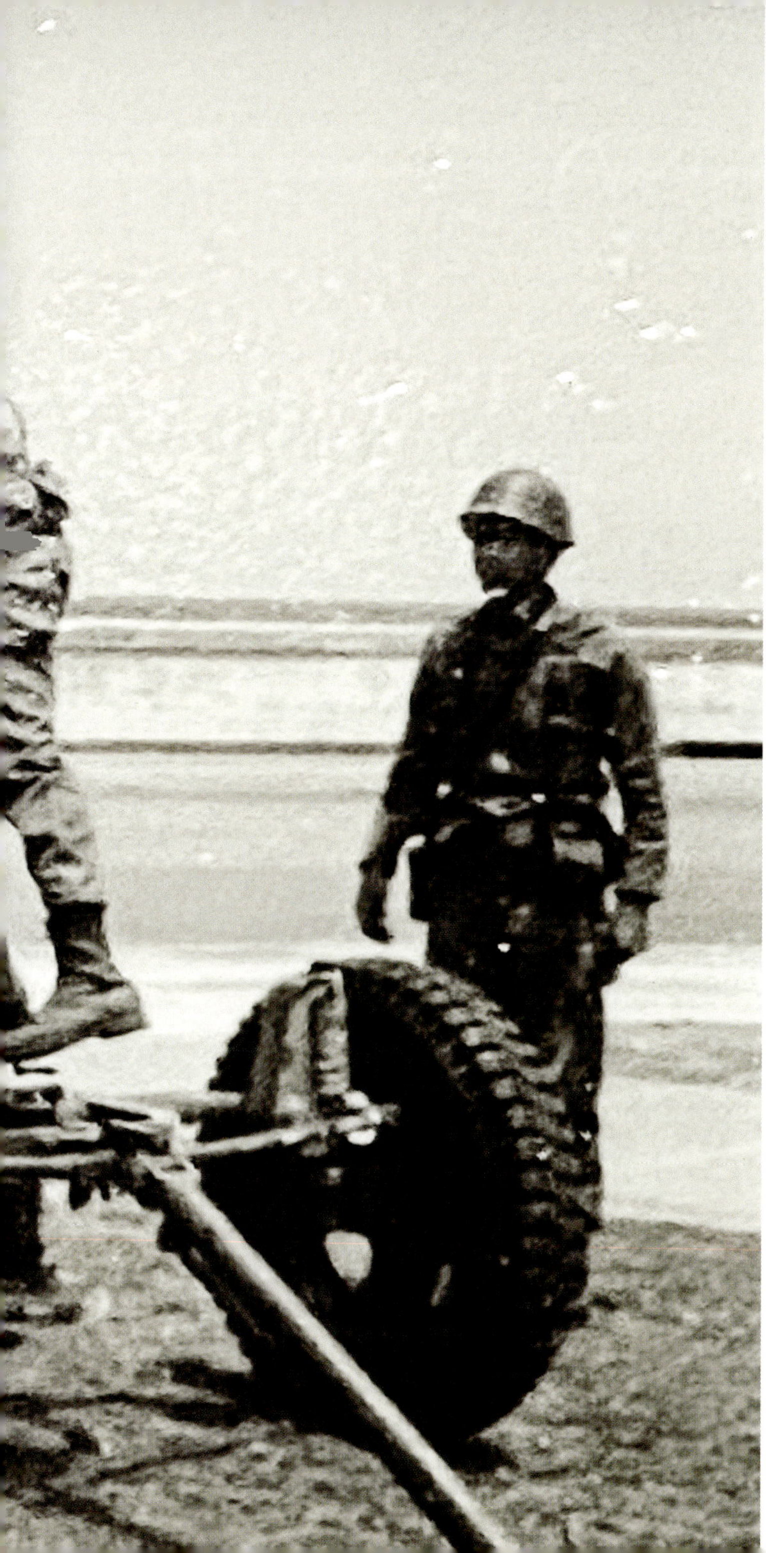

26 OCTOBER. Kennedy orders a dramatic increase in the number of low-level flights over Cuba, seriously affecting the morale of the Cuban military. Castro, kept in the dark on negotiations between the USSR and the US, exasperated by these illegal overflights by American reconnaissance planes, goes against Soviet directives and orders his units to fire on foreign aircraft entering Cuban airspace.

The day following, with nerves fraying, unable to reach General Pliev (who is ill again) and strongly encouraged by the Cuban military – but in direct contravention of his own orders – a Soviet commander in eastern Cuba brings down an American U-2 spy plane with surface-to-air missiles. The pilot is killed. That night, in the White House, Kennedy watches *Roman Holiday* with Mimi Beardsley, his teenage mistress, unable to sleep. Back in Cuba, under the cover of darkness, warheads are delivered from the underground central storage depot to their respective bases.

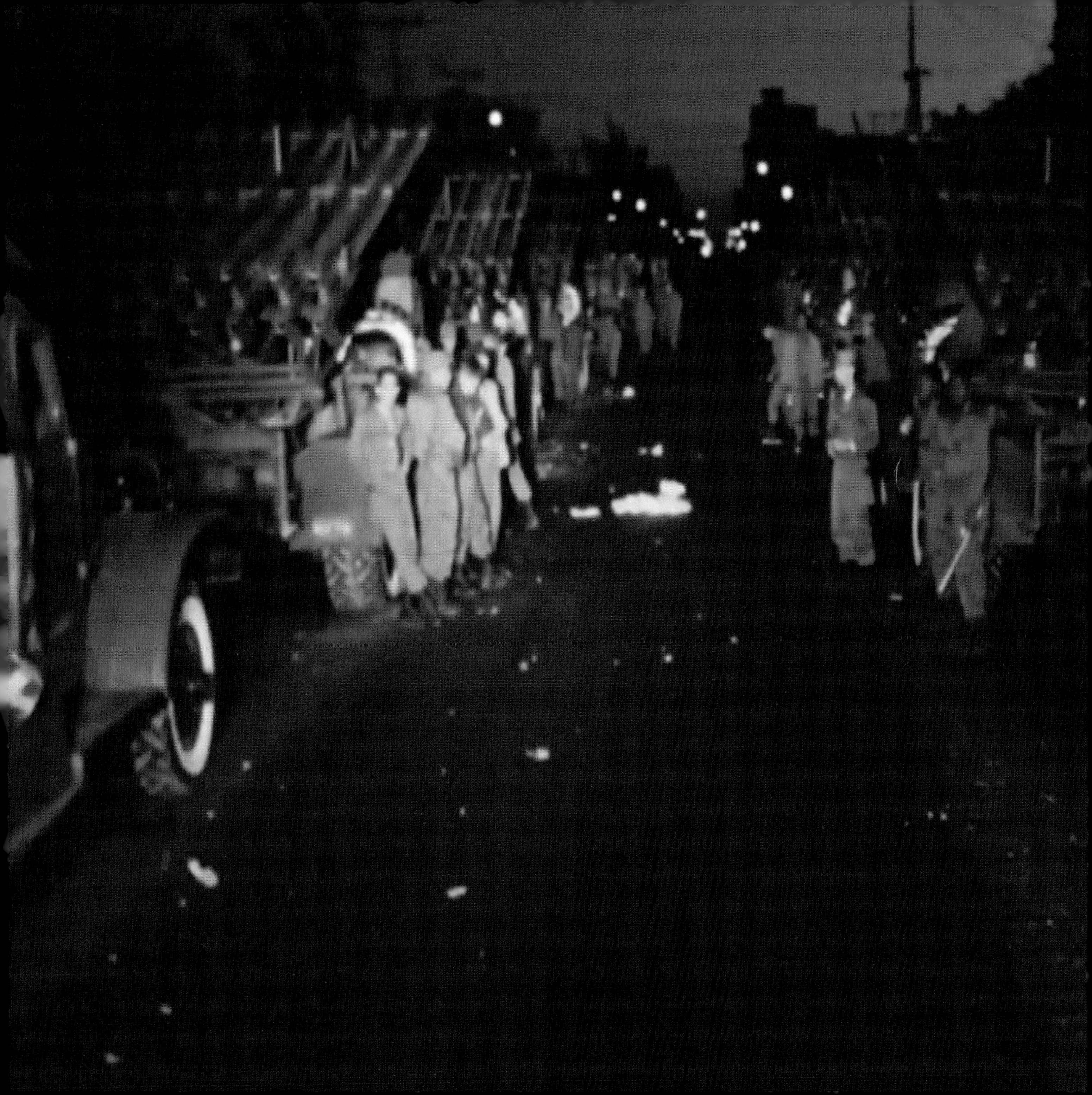

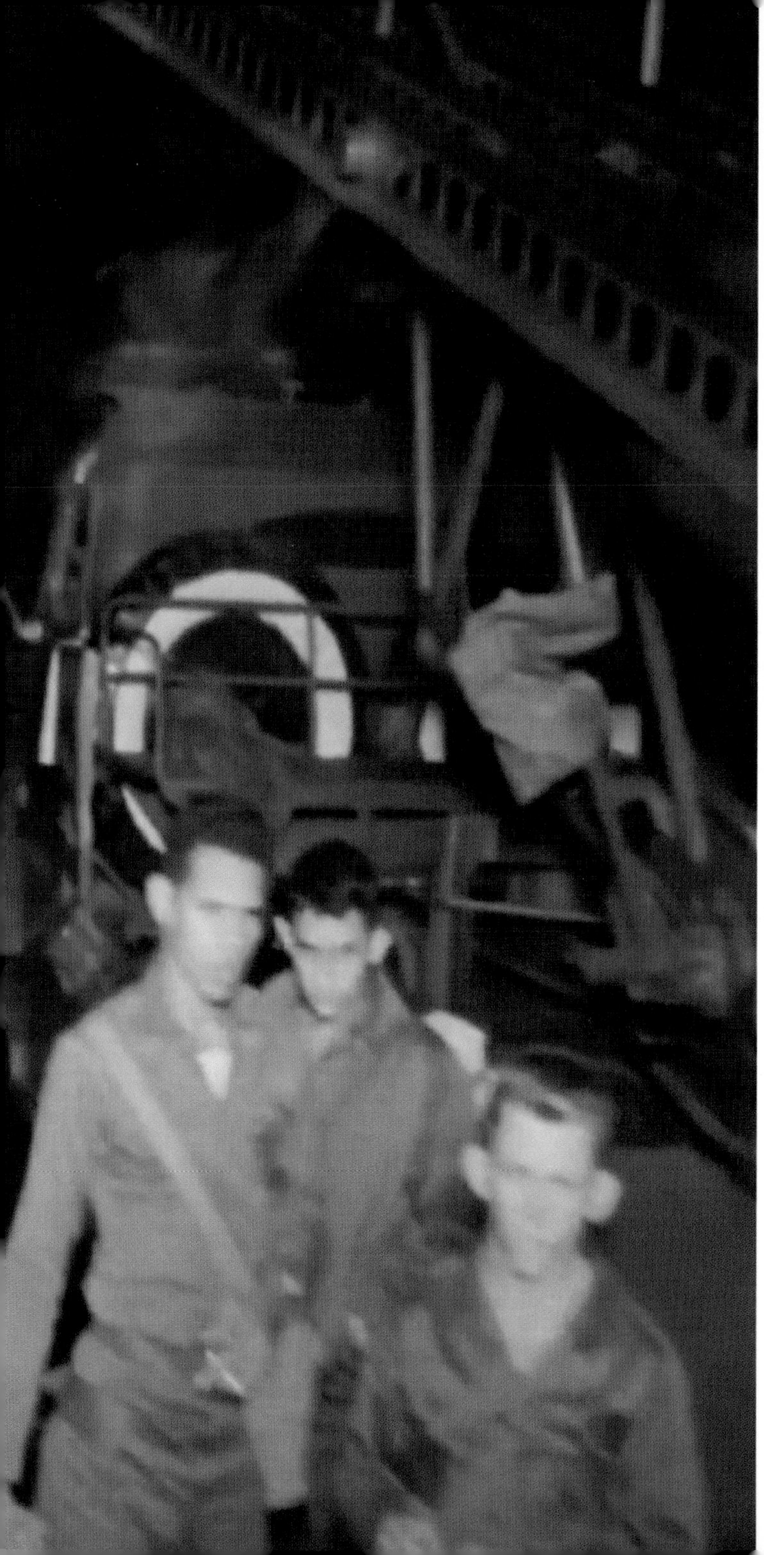

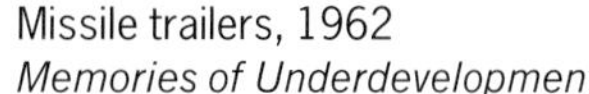

Missile trailers, 1962
Memories of Underdevelopment

The sound of a clock ticking. In the script of *Memories of Underdevelopment*, and the novel by Edmundo Desnoes on which it is based, Sergio and his maid Noemí lie naked in bed, listening to the blues on a Miami radio station when the broadcast is interrupted by the voice of Kennedy.

> **Aggressive conduct, if allowed to go unchecked and unchallenged, ultimately leads to war ... I have directed initial steps to be taken immediately ...**
> **It shall be the policy of this nation to regard any nuclear missile launched from Cuba ... as an attack by the Soviet Union on the United States requiring full retaliatory response.**

She seems not to understand; he, only now becoming aware of the missiles in Cuba, states anxiously that US marines must already be on their way. Sergio, writing in his diary because the clatter of the typewriter strings him out, looks down on Vedado and wonders what it must have been at the turn of the century, green and leafy, the edge of town, before the reinforced concrete hotels all around him were built.

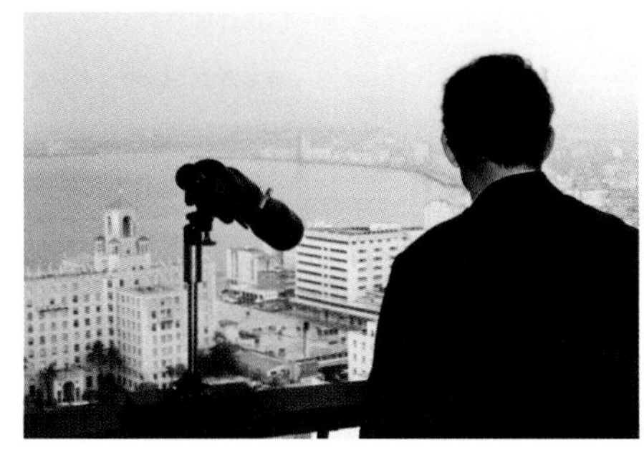

In voiceover, Sergio's thoughts, able to conceive of a shot, a stab wound, even the bursting of a grenade. But he cannot conceive of a city entirely vaporised by an atomic bomb. He is nothing but a cow standing motionless in a field, under the rain. Eisenhower's description of a 'clean bomb' is puritanical hypocrisy, pure and simple. A refrain sounds from Charles Mingus's 'Oh Lord Don't Let Them Drop that Atomic Bomb on Me'.

There are no cracks left, anyway. Protest will do me nothing. We're all in this together. I'll die like all the rest. This island is a trap. We're too small, and too poor. A costly dignity. I don't want to think, don't want to know anything. Nothing.

Sergio looks over the rooftops of Havana, and then at the small Portocarrero painting on his wall: the composition in the painting is far better. He is disdainful of the people he sees below. Castro appears on television, giving a defiant speech; this is intercut with images from the confrontation at the UN, the advance of armoured vehicles, a billowing mushroom cloud. *Never have we been more important, nor more miserable. Ships one day will sail over the spot that was once Cuba, full of nostalgia.* Sergio goes out onto the seafront malecón, where tanks and munition lorries are rolling by, trailers covered in tarpaulin; he wants none of it. The air is heavy, lacking oxygen. A butterfly flapping desperately in a vacant lot. Sergio takes a handful of pills. *And if everything kicks off now? Well, what can I do? I won't try and scuttle into a crack like some cockroach.*

28 OCTOBER. Without consulting the Soviet command, Castro makes public his own conditions for a peaceful solution to the crisis, conditions at odds to those agreed between Khrushchev and Kennedy. One of these prerequisites includes the return of the US naval base at Guantánamo Bay. Kennedy has agreed to remove his Jupiter missiles from Turkey, but this is kept secret.

29 OCTOBER. According to the wishes of the secretary-general of the United Nations, in Cuba brokering negotiations, the Soviets begin to dismantle their bases. As a condition of the agreement, the camps are bulldozed, the launchpads prised out of the ground and blown up; every trace of their presence is to be effaced. Castro refuses to let the UN monitor the process from the ground. Much to the humiliation of the Soviet officers, the missiles are ordered to be displayed dockside to passing planes before being loaded back into the ships, this time in broad daylight. The Cubans learn about the deal through press reports. In a tirade Castro fulminates against Khrushchev, who has no *cojones*, and sets off a chant (already popular on the streets of Havana) through the crowd: *Nikita, mariquita, lo que se da no se quita*, 'Nikita, you little fag, what you give you don't take back'.

2 NOVEMBER. Anastas Mikoyan, who had presided over the first Soviet-Cuban trade relations in 1960, is sent to Havana to try and calm Castro down and persuade him not to derail the delicate withdrawal agreements. He takes with him Eisenstein's *Ivan the Terrible* to watch with the Cuban leader during lulls in negotiations, instruct him in the perils of an abuse of power.

9 NOVEMBER. The last ship carrying R-12s leaves the southern port of Casilda, where they had first arrived over two months before. Unbeknownst to the Americans, who did not learn of this until the 1990s, as a precaution the Soviets do not remove the tactical Luna missiles.

7 DECEMBER. Che Guevara makes a rousing speech in which he repeats the words of Antonio Maceo, the nineteenth century hero of independence: *Whosoever attempts to overpower Cuba, if he does not die in the attempt, will gather merely the dust of her blood-soaked earth.*

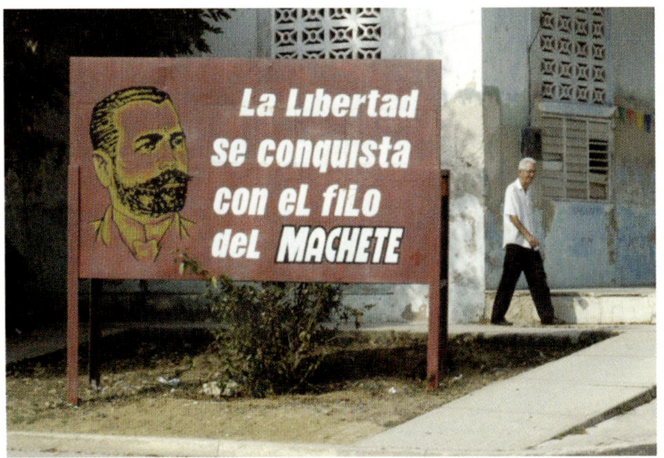

Maceo slogan:
'Freedom is won with a machete'
Antilla, eastern Cuba

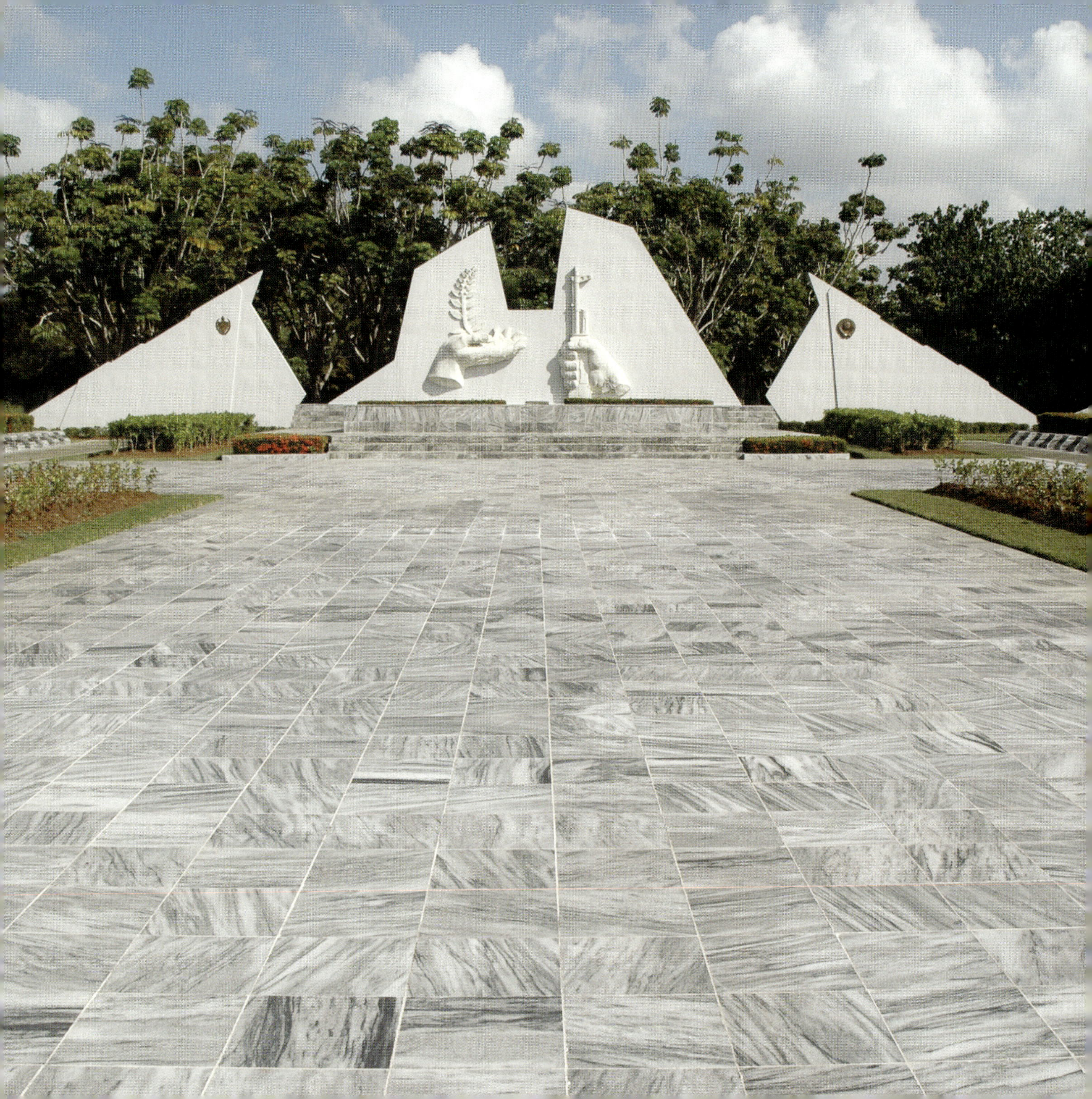

Обращение к потомкам
Заложено 23 II - 1978 г
Вскрыть в день - 150 летия
Советских Вооруженных Сил -
23 II - 2068 г

LLAMAMIENTO A LOS DESCENDIENTES
DEPOSITADO EL 23 02 1978
ABRIR EL 23 02 2068
DIA DEL 150 ANIVERSARIO
DE LAS FUERZAS ARMADAS SOVIETICAS

The Memorial to the Soviet Internationalist Soldier – to the south of Havana – contains 74 tombs of Russian soldiers who died in Cuba (mostly, as locals say, caused by drink-driving accidents). Inaugurated in 1978, to mark the 60th anniversary of the Red Army, an eternal flame flickers above a sealed casket containing a message to their heirs, not to be opened until 2068.

It has been said that Khrushchev's gambit in the Caribbean was a political, if not a strategic, failure and damaged the USSR's standing in the world. Even though he successfully achieved the removal of the US nuclear missiles in Turkey, this was not made public immiediately. And he may well have averted another US invasion of Cuba. But, in the end, Khrushchev's decision to deploy the missiles in secret (against the wishes of some, including the Cubans) in the mistaken belief they would not be discovered, hastened his removal from the post of First Secretary exactly two years following the Missile Crisis.

Mikhail Gorbachev negotiated the withdrawal of the last 11,000 Russian troops from Cuba in 1991, as the Soviet Union fell apart. Once again, the Cuban government was not consulted on what was, in essence, a bilateral agreement between the US and Russia. Vladimir Putin renewed relations with Cuba on a visit in the year 2000, but a year later – following the 11 September terrorist attacks – decided to close down Russia's remaining spy base to the south of Havana. Returning to the island in 2014, Putin visited the Memorial to the Soviet Internationalist Soldier and wrote off 90% of Cuba's debt to his country; rumours soon began to circulate about the planned reopening of Russia's electronic surveillance station.

In January 2022, less than one month before his country's invasion of the former Soviet republic, Russia's deputy foreign minister threatened to deploy 'military assets' to Cuba if the US continued to support Ukrainian sovereignty. In April of the same year a predictable, if depressing, news item ran in *Granma* – the Cuban government's mouthpiece – denouncing reports of the murder of Ukrainian civilians at Bucha as 'fabrications and falsehoods'. In July Andrei Gurulyov, a Russian politician speaking on state television, advocated stoking a new Cuban Missile Crisis by moving supersonic weapons within striking distance of the US.

It is widely believed that Russia has been increasing the amount of tactical nuclear weapons it has in its arsenal recently. As the reader will notice, most of the armaments sent to Cuba in 1962 came from locations in present-day Ukraine, places – for the most part east of the Dnieper – which have become widely known in 2022 for the most tragic of reasons. That Okhtyrka, Lebedyn – once regimental bases of the Soviet 43rd Missile Division – and Mykolaiv should be devastated by Russian missiles sixty years later lends eerie and troubling resonances to this anniversary year.

Richard Hollis

What prompted me to go to Cuba? Simply, that news of an attempt to build a new society made me curious. My politics, in retrospect, were late-19th century: not Marxist, but Tolstoyan; a William Morris-infused, woolly Kropotkin-esque anarcho-socialism. Liberal, CND, naturally. Through someone at the London School of Economics, known to my first wife Tasha Kallin (who died in 1968), I obtained an introduction to the poet Pablo Armando Fernández at Casa de las Américas, who eventually put me on to José Rodríguez Feo and Tony Évora. The latter became a friend. Tony had come from advertising and started out as a graphic designer working for the novelist Guillermo Cabrera Infante at <u>Lunes de Revolución</u>. Later, he designed several book covers for works by Castro.

The airline ticket for my return to Prague proved useless. Cuban regulations required visitors to leave by the same means by which they arrived. The speediest sea route was via New York. We were greeted – in transit from a country under both trade embargo and naval blockade – with the words WORLD PEACE THROUGH WORLD TRADE. I was anxious to get back to Europe and had to write an apology for absence to Lawrence Gowing, Principal of Chelsea School of Art.

There was a coda to the travelogue. My experiences in Cuba seemed of great interest to three grey-suited men on reaching La Coruña, Spain. I was escorted to a cabin and politely grilled. What had I seen? There was no reason to object to the question and my answers were frank. Yes, I'd seen Russians; and I'd seen Soviet boats. Of course, I had no idea at the time as to why they were so keen on this particular item of information. I didn't draw any attention, as a foreigner taking pictures. But I decided, to my subsequent regret, to discard a roll of film I'd shot on a tour of Havana's port.

I was saddened by the memory of seeing those families on the docks, divided by exile. And I was concerned by what I heard about the workings of the Committees for the Defence of the Revolution (CDRs), a version of which

I'd already seen in action in Tunisia. During my stay, an unidentified ship had directed cannon fire at Havana. I have no idea whom it was who questioned me in La Coruña, but I certainly felt the political tensions throughout my trip, without being aware of their magnitude. My hotel room was searched during my stay, and my passport 'kept' for safekeeping. I felt the need to inform the embassy of my movements. At the time, my wife's mother worked as a translator of Russian at the Foreign Office. One day, her boss indicated to her a substantial file on his desk. 'Your son-in-law's', he said.

Rather than Agnès Varda's '<u>Salut les Cubains</u>', the atmosphere of Cuba in 1962 was better evoked for me in Chris Marker's film '<u>Cuba Si!</u>', screened at the time of my return from the island.

A version of my own text, reproduced here, first appeared in the winter of 1962, not long after my return to London. The idea of printing anything about my visit to Cuba arose only a month or two after my return. I had kept a notebook, and my wife Tasha gave me a couple of letters I had sent her. These were the basis of the text. The photographs were taken on a Sports Rolleiflex. The broadsheet's title '<u>I, Eye</u>' was intended to both indicate that it was a personal view and to read as if a street yell – ai-ee, aieee! '<u>Albion Broadsheet</u>' no.2 took its title from the building in Clerkenwell where I was living and working at the time. (There was neither a no.1 nor a successor.) The preparation for printing was painstakingly unprofessional. Photographs had to be first made into screened negatives. The typewritten text was also transformed into negatives. These films were positioned and fixed on an acetate sheet, on a glass-topped table lit from below. From this sheet a lithographic plate was made. One hundred copies were printed. There was no intention of making a profit. Copies were given away, others delivered to a bookshop on Charing Cross Road, to be sold for one penny.

VIVA
CUBA
VIVA LA
PAZ
MUNDIAL

<h1 style="text-align:center;color:#e8491d">ACKNOWLEDGEMENTS</h1>

This book owes a debt to Bruno Mattiussi and Elena Pérez San Miguel. Thanks are due to Pierre Folliet, Nils Longueira Borrego and Jessica Dooling at Yale; the staff and clientele of the Owl Shop provided much sustenance. Sandra del Valle Casals knocked on doors, opened many, and on occasion supplied Cuban home cooking. Will Forrester, Mia Korab, Jasper Ridley and Jessica Sequeira proofread, and substantially improved, our text.

In Cuba, Luciano Castillo Rodríguez and Daymar Valdés Frigola at the Instituto Cubano del Arte e Industria Cinematográficos (ICAIC) were of great help with images and permissions for *Memories of Underdevelopment*. Håkan Karlsson: thank you for your expertise and introductions; and, likewise, to Javier Iglesias Camargo, travelling companion and researcher. As ever, to Mercedes Ruíz and Cynthia Garit the deepest gratitude for your hospitality, patience and advice.

The following have kindly given us permission to use copyright material: Andrew Szentgyorgyi and the heirs of Andrew St. George; Manuscripts and Archives, Yale University Library; Laura Palomares, Carina Pons and Nuria Coloma at Agencia Balcells in Barcelona; the John F. Kennedy Presidential Library and Museum.

Further debt is owed to Luc Chessex who generously sent us photographs and granted permission for their use. The assistance of Ian Denning, Ali Musa at MacMedicine and Christopher Wilson for technical and typographic help has been invaluable.

We are also grateful to Rebecca Carter at Janklow & Nesbit UK; and, of course, to our publisher Ross Bradshaw, and Pippa Hennessy, from Five Leaves.

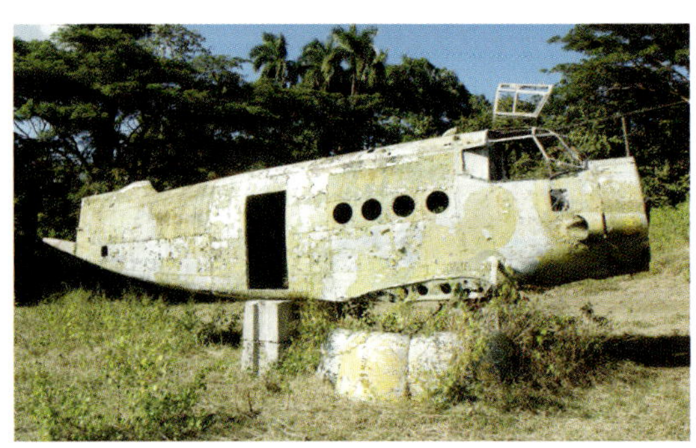

Fuselage, Soviet Antonov, El Cacho
2019